T0198876

SUCH IS LIFE

By

Michael Pulman

Order this book online at www.trafford.com
or email orders@trafford.com

Most Trafford titles are also available at major online book retailers.

Printed in the United States of America.

ISBN: 978-1-4269-8942-1 (sc)
ISBN: 978-1-4269-8943-8 (e)

Trafford rev. 08/26/2011

 www.trafford.com

North America & international
toll-free: 1 888 232 4444 (USA & Canada)
phone: 250 383 6864 ♦ fax: 812 355 4082

Contents

Introduction

My name is Michael Pulman and I am from the wonderful country of New Zealand. I am 19, a writer and a very keen video maker. I love almost everything that life throws at me especially sport and of course my wonderful family. But I live life with a difference to most other people as I am physically disabled and live my life in a wheelchair. It has been one hell of a journey in the nineteen years I have lived so far, some has been great and some has been frankly horrible. Join me as a take a look back at what some may say is a difficult life, I say it's a great challenge and I feel honoured to have lived it. From when I was born, through good times and bad, this is my story of the journey of a disabled person growing up in the awesome country of New Zealand. I will talk about the sometimes harsh realities of being a disabled person and will reveal some secrets that no one has heard until now. I very much hope you enjoy my book and thank you very much for taking the time to read it.

Chapter 1: December, The Month Of Joy

The month of December is always the most joyful and celebrated month of the year. Just a week out from Christmas on the 17th of December in the year 1991 I was born and it was not in the most usual of circumstances. Probably one of the major reasons I am like I am was due to the fact that I was two months premature which in many cases when a baby is this early they often do not survive. I was born early and weighed only 1200g, which I am told is very tiny. The big story of my birth was that I am adopted. My birthmother of whom I have never met was not aware that she was pregnant and when I was born it came as quite a shock to her and her immediate family, it must be tough when out of nowhere you have a baby and you are not emotionally or mentally prepared for it. I know a lot of readers will be wondering how my birthmother did not know she was pregnant with me, well all I know is I was a very tiny baby and I did not move inside the whom. If you couple this with the fact that she was in her early 40s it is not a surprise that these things occurred and in my opinion anyway this is a major reason why I am disabled. Not many people know that I am an adopted child and well I have kept it that way because so many people just cannot understand the process and how it feels to be an "adopted child" when really it is just a straightforward as when a child lives with their birthparents. I have never met my birthmother or my birthfather and to be honest it has never bothered me in the slightest, the saying goes how can you want or miss something that you have never known about. As I understand it my birthmother is called Linda and she was a very successful lady who ran her own business, as for my birthfather there is virtually no record of him and he passed away shortly after I was born and I do not have any information on him. One thing is though that my birthfather was from Te Kuiti, which is where I have lived my entire live and still live here to this day. So I guess I am from the great region of Te Kuiti and I have always had a very great respect for this town, it may be a little town in New Zealand that no one has heard of but it is and will always be home for me. With the death of my birthfather I have no idea what he did for a living or what his interests were but I am so happy that he came from my hometown and he was not some city dwelling person. The country offers so much more enjoyment than the cities because you have room to breathe and it does not take hours to get anywhere, take the city of Auckland for example when it takes you three hours from home to work twice a day, I could not live like that for a fleeting second. Of course with cities comes the advantage of more social and work opportunities, which is great, but I will always favour living in the quite country as opposed to the hustle and bustle of the big city. Part of me wishes that I knew what my birthmother did for a living, the fact that she ran her own business seems quite cool and who knows maybe someday I will receive a big cheque in the mail from her when she passes away as I am made aware that she did not have any other kids and seen as though she was in her early 40s I doubt very highly that she would have had more kids following my unexpected birth. I would be telling a lie if I said I have never been curious into meeting my birthmother but honestly I am happy with how things are 19 years on and I consider my parents Nannette and Lew my true 100% parents and they have done a better job raising me than any other parent of parents could even attempt to do. Having said that I don't know what the future holds and who knows maybe some day I will meet her or she will contact me, but for now I am very happy and have no intention of making contact. Some people may think that is not the best way to go about things but as I said I am very happy with my family and I love them very much. So I was born around two months early. From what mum and dad have said to me it seems my birthmother had a very tough time deciding what to do when I was born, remembering that fact that she did not know that she was carrying me I cannot imagine the confusion that she must have felt in the month of December 1991. It took her around month to decide wether she would adopt me out or not and I imagine with a heavy heart she chose to put me up for adoption. In case you were wondering my original name was Christopher Michael. My birthmother's name was Linda if you were wondering. So following my shock birth I spent the next 7 weeks of my early life in an incubator at Waikato Hospital in Hamilton, my birthmother came and saw me every day for the first few weeks as I am sure she was trying to decide what to do. I was a very tiny baby and had bright red hair. Around this time my parents Nannette and Lew were planning on adopting a child and the adoption agency got in contact with my parents in the month of February 1992 and before you knew it they were on their way to the hospital. In my opinion people who can have their own children take it for granted as the adoption process can take months if not years for a keen parent or parents to find a child. So one day my parents were at work when the adoption agency rang my mother and told them something had opened up and could they possibly get to Hamilton as quick as possible. My parents were very excited about this and they quickly got my older sister, Jenna out of school and were in the car on the way to the hospital. My sister was very much into her schoolwork and was not impressed to have been taken out of school but when Mum and Dad told her that the three of them were going to get Jenna a little brother she was jumping for joy. When a family adopts a child there is a big long legal process that you have to go through, from what I know the adoption lady that worked with my parents was very good at her job and that makes me happy knowing that my parents worked with a total professional. So it was off to Hamilton and my sister could not possibly be more excited. When they got to Waikato Hospital they were greeted by the adoption agency and it was off to the "baby room" as the hospital called it, and I was in a room with around 20 other babies that were also up for adoption. My sister was very clear in the fact that she was not leaving the hospital without her little brother, she was very young back then but the same dominant attitude lives to this day, if anyone messes with her little brother then there is going to be serious trouble. So Jenna saw a wee baby with red hair and my family decided that they would be taking me home and that was it. From what I understand the nurses were very sad to see me go, as I was a very popular baby in the adoption unit. So in less than a week Mum, Dad and Jenna had gone from the three of them to adding another addition to the family, which is great. I should clarify that the "baby room" was full of early born babies that were up for adoption, can you imagine walking into a room and here is a whole lot of wee babies in incubators it would be awesome wouldn't it??? My new family named me Michael Lewis Pulman and the only memory I have of my birthmother is a little circular item that you hang on the wall with the name Christopher Michael on it. I am glad that Mum and Dad kept the name Michael and I don't know the reason why but I am sure it was out of respect for my birthmother, it would not surprise me because that's the type of people my parents are, very caring soul of the earth folk. To be precise my family came and saw me on one day and then sorted out all the paperwork and then brought me home from the hospital the next day. When Mum and Dad first laid eyes on me apparently I was making a hell of a noise because like babies very often are I was hungry and wanting a feed. My parents and my older sister were over the moon to have a baby boy in the family. In the following weeks after my adoption the lady from the adoption agency made regular visits to make sure everything was going ok and a few months later my parents completed the adoption process and the courts made it all official. The adoption agency lady told my parents that the most important thing a parent can do is be just as strict as if it were your own biological children. It was also made clear that I would have the right to meet my biological parents when I was old enough to make my own decisions. Surprisingly the process after adoption does not last that long and we were the perfect happy family living in the country town of Te Kuiti in no time. The first year if my life was relatively simple, my sister absolutely loved having a brother and she did everything with me. I was a very small baby as I weighed only 1200g at birth and you could fit my entire body in the palm of an adults hand I was so tiny, there were so many memories from the early days. There is a eight year age gap between my sister and I and she was skiting to all her friends at school saying things like "I have a little brother and he is so cool" before I even was at the age to go to school she went around telling her friends and other students that "my brother is coming to this school soon" and various other things like that. Mum and Dad tell me she was very proud of me and had to tell everyone about her cute little brother.

Jenna was very good when I was a baby, no one was more happy than her when she found out that she would be having a little brother and as you can imagine at that age Mum and Dad got a lot of questions about when I was coming and various other questions, its cute it really is. It must have been a change for Jenna too as it had been just her and my parents for the seven years previous but she took to it like water on a ducks back and I am thankful for that. The first year of my life consisted as it does for all baby's, sleeping and eating. Dad used to race home from work and I would always seem to be awake when he would come through the door and we would have a lot of fun, he would pick me up and fly me around the room well I would be laughing my young lungs out. It is memories like this that are priceless, not that I remember much of it mind you as I was just a baby. As a baby I loved doing anything with either my parents or my sister, be it walks in the park or trips to the grocery store, I was a relative active baby. A lot of babies at an early stage are difficult to try and get too feed at times and I was the same, some days I would be a darling when it came to having a feed and others I would not want to eat or drink anything at all. Mum and Dad say that I slept well and was a very well behaved baby and did not have too many early problems, the first year of a child's life is very crucial to there development and the way parents approach things will determine a lot. My parents did a lot with me, Im sure all the baby games took place in our house. We were so happy and I had the best childhood that any kid could possibly ask for, supportive parents, a safe environment and everything was provided for me like toys and of course food which to this day is one of the most important things in my life because hey we cannot live without our food. I love all food especially my Mums homemade queen cakes and her bacon and egg pie. My parents did so much for me throughout the years and I very much appreciate it, it is fair to say that these days the same attitude towards parenting has changed and parents are not as hands on with their children. Please don't get me wrong there are great parents out there but with the recent trend of "kids" having their own kids some lack the maturity to work out the crucial aspects of being a parent, a confidence to a child is everything and is very important as they grow up. Also a happy childhood is crucial because I have found that when you are happy at either a young age or a elder age you can achieve things that you set your mind to. However back to my childhood now, Mum and Dad would often be at work and they would have family come and look after me. Mum was a nurse at Te Kuiti hospital for 25 years and she was one of the best at her job at the time whilst back in those days Dad worked in the forestry industry doing several different jobs. Mum worked 3 – 4 days of the weeks whilst Dad worked full time and travelled to work everyday, of course Jenna was in school everyday and would race home to play with me after a long day of school. If you were wondering at all Jenna went to Te Kuiti Primary School, which is known as the most popular and successful primary school in the district. With my Mum being a nurse for 25 years, the skills and knowledge she had would prove to be very important in the years to come as we discovered my disability and it would begin to take effect on my physical ability. Various members of the family would look after me, from close friends to auntie's and more my childhood was just great. There were so many good times that I have been made aware of from when I was a baby, I would wrestle around on the floor with dad and we would both have a ball of a time. My dad just loves children and I know this because he is a very popular poppa now days as my sister Jenna has had two children over the last few years. I loved most usual things that a baby likes, I had a real passion for the television programme "Thomas And The Tank Engine" and to this day I still enjoy watching that famous kids programme. I also enjoyed all the classic movies like "The Little Mermaid" plus "Beauty And The Beast" the list goes on and on and again to this day I will sit down and watch these movies because they are pure classics. Mum was telling me that because I could not walk or crawl I would roll around on the floor and it may take me sometimes half an hour to reach or grab something but I would not be outdone. Determination is something that to this day I take very seriously and I will never give up on anything I put my mind to. Mum was very busy not only working but doing things with my sister too so naturally in the early stages I would have more playtimes with dad who was also very busy but we always found time to do things as a family. My sister Jenna would cart me around the house, as she was determined that her little brother was going to do everything with her. She would also read me hundreds of books when it came to bedtime throughout the years, she would even read me her school homework and reports, which is very cute. Jenna would play with all my toys with me and we would wrestle around on the floor like I would with dad, Jenna had to be involved in every aspect of my young life. I had a very small bed or cot when I was a baby and it was very low down to the floor so that if for some reason I would move around I would not fall out of bed. My parents did not take any measure too simply when it came to their son and daughter they were very much "on the safe side" parents which it the best way to be. I loved my soft toys as all babies do, my aunty brought me a big and soft light blue teddy bear that went everywhere with me when I was a baby. For the life of me I cannot remember the name of this teddy but I still love that teddy to this day. Some people may read this and think I am a little bit of a girl but when you're a kid it is the simple things that you love more than anything in the world like books or soft toys, as my mum says quite often to me about my baby nephews is that it does not take much to keep a baby entertained and I was no exception. My days consisted of sleep, feeding and playing around on the floor with my various beloved toys. One of the things I am most proud is what I called my "blanky" which is a very special blanket that was knitted for me by my grandmother on my dad's side. All four of my grandparents were good to me and I had a good relationship with all of them, my grandma on my mum's side would slip me $5 every time I saw here and my poppa Bob had a model railway in his garage which is amazing to me every time I see it. I will talk about this a little later on in this book. Early from the outset there were signs though that there was potentially something just a little bit different about me, I had trouble doing a lot of things that most babies would not have any trouble doing at this stage. Now doubt down to the fact that I was so tiny when I was born, remembering the fact that I weighed just 1200g in birth some problems were bound to arise down the track. After a wee while mum and dad noticed that I had a bit of trouble feeding and when I got to the stage of having foods like Wheetbix and more a dietary supplement was needed, as I was not getting enough food in my system. I would have a walker and although I could not take wait through my legs it helped a lot in getting me around the house when most babies would be beginning to walk at this stage. Again the determination that I had was not to be outdone, it might take me half an hour to grab something I knew I was not supposed to have but like most babies I went ahead and tried anyway. There was no difference to other kids it would just take me a little bit longer to do things than others, a trend that would become the norm later on in life. The fact that I could not crawl and after several attempts I could not take wait through my legs I am sure mum and dad were starting to get worried but it is a difficult situation to find yourself in because often babies develop physical ability at different times and situations, not every baby is the same so my parents were at a stage of waiting to see. When mum worked as a nurse she worked with a lot of babies and through that experience was getting more and more concerned as the weeks past, it must be hard for a parent when they have a young baby who is not developing as quick as most other kids and you don't know why it is happening and may think that you are just being a nervous parent. I would be sitting or playing on the floor and my parents would watch and as the months went on the discussions began that possibly a trip to the doctor was necessary. So within a few days an appointment with the doctor was made and to my parents surprise the doctor said that something was not quite right and then all of a sudden we were put onto a specialist paediatrician from Hamilton. I wonder how my biological mother would have dealt with all this if she had not have adopted me out but I know for sure that she would not have dealt with it in the positive way that mum and dad did. So begins a very long but crucial journey of tests and appointments that would prove crucial in my diagnosis and indeed my life.

Chapter 2: Tests, Diagnosis, And Opinions

Things can change very quickly in the space of a year, I think it is fair to assume that we all know that and that saying has appealed to us during some part of our lives no matter how old or young you may be. After a while of thinking and pondering my parents decided it was time to make a trip to the doctor, and it was the beginning of a long but very important phase of my young life. The first time we went to see the doctor they could not recognise anything wrong or different with me, which as you can assume did not make my parents feel any better about things, naturally a parent worries it is just the way human nature goes. So after the doctor could not find anything wrong my parents were left feeling less than reassured. My parents and in particular my mother just knew in her gut that something was just not right here and the fact that I had a lot of difficulty feeding and that I could never take weight on my legs it does not take a super smart person to recognise these symptoms. So after a few further visits to the doctor it was finally realised that yes something just is not quite normal here and we were referred to a paediatrician who is a medical professional that is trained in this field. This then lead us to a situation of medical appointments and a whole lot more, however the first paediatrician we dealt with was less than supportive and was not the most professional medical person in the world. The first time we met this man he said the following to my mother "You mothers!!! You expect everything to happen at once!!!" to say this to a parent that is already in a very nervous and anxious state is as about as far south as you can go from a professional and that comment really hurt my mother, it stayed with her for a very long time and if I saw that man again I would have something to say to him myself. It was very frustrating because the signs of physical disability were very clear at this stage and yet our first paediatrician could not pick up on that. Naturally mum and dad were not impressed in the slightest so we got referred to another paediatrician and it was there that the process of tests and many, many medical appointments began. That is the funny thing about a neuromuscular condition, it's that early on even the people in the highest of medical fields cannot recognise the symptoms. The entire journey I have been on has been a process of trial and error of a lot of things, be it new innovative drugs that people want you to try right through to having major surgeries, in the early days it was very much trial and error and that trend has continued to this day and will no doubt continue well into the future, its almost fun to go through in a way whilst at other times it can be a right pain in the backside. I really admire my parents and in particular my mother for not giving up when in the early stages she basically got told she was being paranoid by people who call themselves professionals, she didn't give up and I think she just knew in her heart that she had to do something and make her case heard. It is actually quite often the case we have found through the years, you have to make things happen because even in some of the highest medical fields people will not go the extra mile if they do not need too and we found this to be the case with several paediatricians we dealt with in the very early stages of diagnosis. So after a wee while of meeting new people and finding that no they didn't have an answer for our concerns we finally found the right paediatrician and he would become a major part of our journey for the next eighteen years and I can tell you this man is one of the most professional and well respected person in his field and is commonly known as one of the very best in this country at what he does. So without a doubt we had hit the jackpot here, this man not only went the extra mile medically but he was and has been a great support to my parents and myself over the years, advice is something that is golden. Now the original possibility that these people thought could be wrong with me was they thought that I might have what's called 'Seribal Pausy', this is a hard disability to explain, it is both mental and a slightly physical disease and a lot of people in New Zealand do have this disability, however that possibility was blown out of the water when I began to talk a few weeks later. People who have 'Seribal Pausy' cannot speak it is one of the crucial parts of the disease. So then it was back to hospital for further appointments and tests as we tried to figure out what this damn thing was, by this time we knew that something was different here but we did not know what it was and that was the scary thing for my parents. All this did not have any effect on me because after all I was a baby and at that age all you care about is sleep and when the next round of food is coming, sometimes you wish life was still like that even today especially when certain aspects of your life may not be going the way that you want them too, I think we would all like things to be a little more simple from time to time. What we all realise however is that life is not always plain sailing and we deal with every challenge of every day as it comes, I believe the way we respond to challenges that life throws at us is what makes us who we are. So it was back to square one for us and it was at this point that my parents came to their first and very tough realisation that would become more and more prominent over the years. It is actually something that as the child I cannot really grasp, it was at this point that Mum and Dad kind of realised that they could not fix this unknown problem that their child was having, and I believe it was at this point that they got the message that I might possibly not live the "normal" life that every other kid lives without any physical problem. When I say that I mean as in not a physical problem that is not going to go away and if anything it could get worse in the future especially considering the situation we were all of a sudden in. You may have found that last sentence confusing, what I mean is most kids around the world don't have a disease that kills there physical ability, granted almost every kid will hurt themselves on various occasions throughout there life be it a broken leg or whatever but a lot of them will not have a physical limitation to live with for a lifetime. That is all I am saying, sometimes people take for granted what they have never had to worry about like the ability to walk. Whilst my parents may have been feeling a bit powerless for a while there it is really interesting because my sister Jenna appeared to take the entire thing in her stride, but also I am not sure how much she knew about the whole situation during these early stages. It is funny actually, her and I think a lot differently today about the disability where as I have come to terms with it and accepted it I am not sure if she has. We have never really discussed it, I have had many conversations with mum and dad about my situation but when it comes to Jenna it has never really come up, at all really if memory serves me right. So where are we??? Oh yes back to the early stages of my life. Whilst Jenna took everything in her stride im sure mum and dad were very worried about things at this point. After the theory that I might have had "Seribal Pausy" was blown away, the various medical professionals that were working with us were back to the stage of trying to recognise the symptoms and get some concrete information about this at that time unknown issue I was having. It was at this point when one of the worst ever things happened to me and my family, it caused stress and I believe is the reason why I have had a life long fear of a medical procedure that thousands of people have everyday around the world. We were put on to a neurologist who is a very advanced professional who deals with a whole lot of things with people who have both physical and mental disabilities. We have dealt with many neurologist's over the years because as you get older you move onto more experienced neurologist's who can deal with various situations that may arise as you get older. Lets just say the first neurologist we ever dealt with was in my opinion the worst person I have ever dealt with in this entire journey. I was three years old at this stage and it was a big turning point in my diagnosis. The doctors around me and my family decided that it would be necessary for me to undergo what is called a "muscle biopsy" which is basically a muscle test but it is more in depth than I am sure a lot of people reading this can imagine. This basically involved me having to lie down on a bed at Waikato Hospital whilst a doctor subjected my body to needle injection after needle injection. Now when I say he gave me and injection everywhere in my body I mean everywhere on my body, from head to toe almost. This is the single only reason why to this day I have a fear of needle injections, I can't even go and get a simple flu injection without worrying myself crazy about the prospect of having an injection. Back to the muscle biopsy. I was just three years of age when this event took place keep that in mind. The neurologist came in the room and barely even said hello to either my parents or myself and he proceeded to give me many painful injections. Today I can still remember the pain I felt that day and it is not a experience that I want to go through again, in fact I will not go through it again not if it is like that experience was I can tell you that beyond a shadow of a doubt. Now I have to say this because I believe it is crucial to the story, the neurologist was a foreign doctor and I can tell you from a lifetime's worth of experience of dealing with so very many people in the medical field, the approach of caring for the patients is a lot different with foreign doctors compared to Kiwi doctors I can tell you. It is actually something that's true in all aspects of life; some people will go the extra mile for you whilst others will only do the bare minimum. Considering this muscle biopsy was my first real hardcore medical exam it could have been dealt with a lot better from the neurologist because he had no tact or even manners throughout the entire ordeal. This is how it went down. The neurologist walked into the room and barely even introduced himself and he made absolutely no attempt to explain to me what he was about to do and he did not explain to my parents either which you would think would be the norm for someone to do but it was not the norm for this guy. For the next ten minutes the neurologist performed the biopsy and I proceeded to scream because I was under the most extreme of pain. When I was talking to mum and dad about this they said that they felt extremely powerless and had to watch their child go through pain that they have never seen me go through before. Dad was very upset and it took all of his energy and being not to deck the man!!!! Its moments like these that will stay with me forever. The guy had no compassion and absolutely zero empathy for me or my family. It gave me such a scare that it took mum and dad a very long time to calm me down and whilst I was very upset the doctor did not apologise or give any reason whatsoever as to why he did what he just did. After all the muscle biopsy had to be done but we did not know what was involved and you would think a professional person like the neurologist would have a little more empathy and understanding than that. Mum was telling me when I was doing some research and notes for this book that after I had been through that horrible ordeal mum and dad were both left very upset as they had just seen me scream in pain for around ten minutes and whilst they wanted nothing more than to make it go away they had no choice but to stand back and let the doctor do his job because this muscle biopsy was very necessary but still you can understand how hard it must have been for them to watch that. There have only been two times in my entire life that my father has come close to decking someone and this was the first, I really admire him for not giving in to his anger and just stepping back because I know if I was in the same situation myself I would not be able to just sit back and watch that happen to my kid. Again it is something I think must be the hardest thing for a parent is to trust another human being with the welfare of your child. It was also an awaking for myself in a lot of ways even though I was only three years of age, I think as it was the first proper medical test of many that I would have throughout my life it gave me a bit of a scare no doubt. The method of this man could and should have been a lot better than was displayed and I know that you just don't treat patients like that, maybe if he had of just explained to my parents and myself what he needed to do it may have gone a lot better but instead of doing that he just walked into the room and began poking me with needles, I will let you the reader decide if you think that is professional or not. To put it into simple terms a muscle biopsy is a test that is done to measure the available muscle strength a patient has and it can be done in several different ways, I just got the most painful way possible but through it all I do understand why I had the test and I am thankful to have had it recommended to me. I know what I think about that man though and you can imagine what I mean by that. Despite it being one of the most painful things a young child could go through these muscle biopsy's proved very critical and a few weeks later we were once again on the way up to Hamilton for further appointments. After a few weeks of talks and recommendations from various medical professionals it was decided that I would join a place called Conductive Education for the next couple of years and everyone seemed to be very positive about the whole thing so mum and dad decided yes I would enrol in this school like program in Hamilton. It meant that I would be travelling to Hamilton three to four days a week for this special school. It was very interesting though as the school was designed more people with diseases like Seribal Pausy and more but the professionals thought that my body would benefit from the physical regime that this school boasts and it is one of the only "disability focused" schools in the country. Like everything my parents were sending me to this school not knowing what to expect but like everything in life at times you just got to run with it and take a chance it could work out badly or it could be the best thing to do. I went to conductive education from the age of two all the way up to beginning primary school at age five so it was a good three years or so that I attended. However before I got granted into the school I had to undergo an assessment with them to determine wether or not my body would be able to cope with the day to day physical work that it would be subject too for the next few years. It was decided that I would be accepted into a special programme that would involve everything from walking to even the most basic of physical workout three to four times of every week. So after a few weeks of waiting for a place to come up it was off to Hamilton every week and I think we were all shocked at just the amount of physical work I would have to do on a day to day basis. Your probably wondering this, if I have a physical disability that decreases my muscles and there is nothing you can do about that then why would we bother taking me to this school, wouldn't it just tire my muscles out even quicker??? Well im sure my parents had that way of thinking in the early stages but the great thing about this school was the people that worked with me and they knew exactly what to do to make that not happen. The funny thing about this is, when most two year olds would be out playing and going to kindergarten I was going to rehab. That's what conductive education was too it was pure 100% physical rehab. Not many two year olds would have to do that, but that's what is so good looking back whilst I write this book is the experiences that I have had. No matter how difficult or easy these experiences were for me I look back and smile because it has all helped me become what I am today, confident in my abilities and I know my limitations. The phrase "never give up" and "keep trying" would be something I would learn very quickly over the next few years at conductive education. It was a great but at the same time very difficult experience for me here, if anyone has been through physical rehab they will know what it is like, its not the easiest thing one can do in their lifetime that is for sure. My days at conductive consisted of the following, walking whilst holding onto a ladder like tool for half an hour to an hour, leg and arm exercises, push ups and sit ups, to name a few. A lot of this was also captured on video and I have watched it a couple of times, I remember one shot that I saw was when someone was filming me whilst I was doing some walking exercises and the look on my face is like I am less than impressed to be on camera. Obviously now days I have no problem being in front of the camera as many people reading this book will know. My experience at conductive education was very crucial in my physical development and I cannot say enough for the people who work here and I love them all. I met some life long friends here. The reason behind all these exercises that I did at conductive education was to strengthen and attempt to build my muscles through repetition and although it was a relative long shot it seemed to be working out very nicely for my body. Make no mistake about it though, this disease cannot be fixed but you can do all you can to try and ensure it does not get any worse than it already is. It was the same schedule every day for us kids at conductive education, we would arrive at around 9am and for the next three to four hours we would be in our own individual physical rehabilitation programs, some were hardcore and others were more laid back and not as difficult, it all depended on the individual child's needs and where they were physically in their respective disability. After a morning's filled of physical workout we would normally have story time followed by a sleep before our parents came to pick us up everyday. I had a special friend called Myra at conductive education, she has seribal pausy and before I came along she was struggling with her rehab and once she met myself she seemed to pick up her workload and we became good friends. According to mum I could not go anywhere or do anything at conductive education without Myra being hot on my heels. She actually could not speak but we still managed to find a way to communicate apparently. We would always have our afternoon sleep together and she was very sad when I left for primary school, whilst she had to continue going to conductive education, as she was not as physically capable as I was. I feel sad to her I really do but she was a lot like me as she was very positive about her situation and I admire her for that. These days she is living in Hamilton I believe but am not to sure about that, seeing as though she cannot speak you can understand when I say contact is at times difficult. I understand she is well and happy though so that is great. So after close to three years of conductive education my body was in the best shape that it could possibly have been in and my doctors and everyone were very delighted. It was then time for me too start primary school but we will get to that a little later in the next chapter of this book. I am now what, around five years of age and well we are all happy at this stage, Jenna is looking forward to her brother coming to her school and it was at this time that another major development in my diagnosis was realised. We got a phone call and it was once again off to Hamilton for a crucial and somewhat joyful medical appointment. After close to six years of tests and medical appointments, from muscle biopsies all the way through conductive education and a whole lot more, myself and my parents were told officially that I had been diagnosed with a disease called Spinal Muscular Atrophy or SMA for short. Spinal Muscular Atrophy is a very similar muscle condition to Muscular Dystrophy but fortunately my condition is not nearly as ruthless and horrible as Muscular Dystrophy is and I am very happy about that looking back. At that age I did not really understand but mum and dad were both very happy and almost relieved with the situation. After six years of uncertainty and worrying we finally knew what we were up against and there is something about that which is comforting. However at the same time my parents did feel very concerned and uncertain about what the future would hold for me and if I would have the quality of life that other kids have, it was really a case of now we knew what disability I had and we had to wait and see how it would effect me and I am sure that it would have been a hard pill for mum and dad to swallow. We now knew what we were up against and although a possibility of a bleak outlook we were ready to take the challenge of Spinal Muscular Atrophy by the balls and make life what we wanted it to be. Bring it on!!!!!

Chapter 3: The Middle Years

The middle years of my life were filled with so much fun and to this day they remain some of the fondest memories and I hold them dare to my heart. I did so much during these years, including starting school and some operations to try and further my physical ability. There was chicken pox and a whole lot more, these middle years were very crucial in my development and I love thinking about these memories, when I am down just thinking of all the fun I had back in the day always brings a smile to my face. The first major happening of my middle years was when I got given my first ever wheelchair at age four, it was a little blue manual wheelchair which I would push along. I actually remember almost every detail of this day from when I first got put into the chair to pushing it around the yard outside the wheelchair shop. As I was four years old and had never been in a wheelchair never mind driven one around. It was a very daunting experience for my family and me because in a way it was like a realisation that yes this is where we are at and the disability was beginning to run its course as I had lost the ability too move around. Up until this point I would not crawl but sort of roll around the place. Other than that my parents would carry me everywhere, it is something that all us kids go through when we have a physical disability and lose the ability to move around without some sort of assistance. I was of course just four years old when this happened but I was so excited and loved my racing new blue wheelchair, and it will be in my heart forever as it was my first ever wheelchair. The chair is a classic item I have owned and it is remembered in the picture we have hanging in the lounge with me and my sister that was taken just after I got the chair given to me by a company called Wheelchair Solutions. This was in the year of what, 1995 and Wheelchair Solutions had been around a fair while and back then they were based in a shop just at the bottom of Waikato Hospital, down under the car park there. In my opinion they should still be based there because parking would be a lot easier for one and there is a lot more space at the old workshop. Now days the old base for Wheelchair Solutions is an unused building, which lies underneath the ever changing layout of the massive Waikato Hospital. It is somewhat sad when you see these once great and very busy buildings being put too no use these days and they are just sitting there empty, I believe it is used sometimes for storage of old unused equipment from the hospital but every time I have driven past the building recently it looks empty and unused, very sad in my opinion and I wish it was still being used by Wheelchair Solutions to this day. That is the strange thing about Hospitals you know and especially Waikato Hospital, it is changing all the bloody time. I don't know why but the higher ups at Waikato Hospital always seem to want to change around the layout of the hospital because every time you go there it has been changed in some way. It is known as the biggest hospital in the Southern Hemisphere. I remember when you could park right outside the front entrance of the hospital but now days you drive almost right around the hospital before you reach the new multi level car park, of which it costs a ridicules amount just to park at the bloody hospital, we want to park there not buy the building. No disrespect at all but you can very much tell the car park and driveway has been designed by university students as there is a speed bump every 10 metres which can prove to be very annoying at times but again it is something that you would get used too very quickly. I am a country boy and I am used to and enjoy things being simple, that is life though you know especially in the big city, things change all the time and you can hardly keep up with it. I have spent a large amount of my life in or around Waikato Hospital and I know it like the back of my hand almost, but even I struggle at times. Well back to the story, sound like a good idea? Yes I think so. I began my schooling life at a school called Te Kuiti Primary School and it is known as one of the better schools in the district. I remember my first ever day at school and remember being so excited, my sister made sure that everyone in the entire school knew that her little brother was coming to the school and she wanted it known that if anyone messed with me there would be serious problems. Jenna has always been a very straight up and fiery individual, over the years she has turned it down a wee bit but still I would not want to mess with her. My primary school experiences varied a lot, it did not take very long for the bullying to begin after I started school, it is a shame that my sister was so much older than me because she was in her last year of primary when I began my first. The first two years of primary were awesome and I met some life long friends there, my teachers were awesome and my teacher for my 2nd year was the best and without a doubt the best teacher I had right throughout my schooling life as she was a teacher that really cared about her students and went the extra mile for her students. You find a lot of teachers these days just do the bare minimum and don't follow things up if a student has been away, but they are quite happy to criticise without following things up. I wish I still was in contact with my 2nd year teacher, she was very understanding of my disability and how it may sometimes effect my performance at school whilst most other teachers don't really want to know and have the perception that I should be able to do everything all the other students can do despite the fact I clearly could not, don't get me wrong I did well at most things but there were occasions were I could not keep the pace. So where are we, oh yes the early years of primary school. It was around this time or perhaps just earlier when I had my first of quite a few major operations. It was at this time that I had the horrible tendon release operations where basically the doctor open up your knee and releases the muscle that becomes tight. Let me see if I can try and explain this, underneath both of my knees the muscles are very tight and I have never been able too straighten my legs and I will never be able too do so. This surgery is designed to release the tendon and make the knees more lose and easy to move around, the surgery was done and it did make a difference for my physical structure if that makes any sense. It was a tough few weeks post surgery and the pain just killed me, I remember every time I moved the pain went shooting well up both legs all the way from the knee right up to the hips, I cannot describe how that feels. It was then that I listened to a song that would become one of my more favourite songs in the years to come, have you ever heard a song called Children? My parents introduced the song to me so many years ago but I just love it and although it brings back memories of that first major operation the song just makes me feel happy and pumped up for some reason. Music is a very important part of our lives and we all love music, some people like country and western, others like rap, but we can all relate to the love of music simply because music creates emotion. If any of us are upset music always seems to be the thing that cheers us up, personally I cannot live without music because it is a calming process for myself, if I am angry it calms me down and makes me think of what I could have done better. At times music also gives me an idea for a blog or even a youtube project, in fact I was listening to my iPod jamming out the sounds when I came up with the idea for the MP Show, something that has put my name out there in the world of social media. People love music for different reasons, I love music because it makes me think and I process a lot of my thoughts when listening to music. I listen to music everyday and I would go insane without that. Just if you're wondering my favourite song is "High" by Lighthouse Family. In my opinion music was better back in the day and it wasn't as explicit as it is today, these days you cant get through a song without some sort of sexual mention or hint. Please don't get me wrong there are some great artists today but you will never beat the talent of yesteryear. For me Pink Floyd will be the band that will live forever, you will not see or hear better music than what that great band produced in the mid to late 90s, just amazing and if you ever have the chance to listen to there music I almost 100% agree that you will not in anyway be disappointed. At this early age was when my passion for watching sports really began, I remember being in the kitchen with dad and watching the Blackcaps play in the 1995 Cricket World Cup and ever since then I have obsessed with the game of Cricket and too this day I try and watch every single game our national cricket team plays. Quickly after I also developed a passion for Rugby, I don't actually know why I got so interested in sports. It is like most people, if your father sits down and watches sport you as the child have to be involved in what your parents do or what they are interested in. As a kid I always had to be by my fathers side and I guess that is where I watched my first ever rugby or cricket match and thankfully the passion for sport is still with me today, I just cannot get enough. Watching sport is so interesting because you get too see the competitive streak in an individual person and I love seeing that. I will even watch golf sometimes that is how bloody obsessed I am with sport. I like most sports like Rugby, Cricket, Rugby League and all the rest. My most popular sport though by a country mile is the great game of Cricket, it is in my blood I am sure of it. In my opinion Cricket is the hardest and most entertaining sport on the planet. Every summer I am in front of the television or PC watching and then writing about all the action and I can't say that I ever get bored with it, when your passionate about something you will never ever get bored with it. My greatest memory of cricket will no doubt live through time and it will remain the single most exciting moment of my life for the foreseeable future, it was back in 2007 when the Blackcaps were struggling at 40 – 4 chasing a target of 350 and they came back to win what I believe is the greatest cricket match in history and it took place at what I believe is the best cricket ground in the world, Seddon Park in Hamilton. Speaking of Hamilton, the mighty Waikato has always been a very successful sporting region, and it has hosted some of the biggest sporting events that New Zealand has including the ITM Hamilton 400 on the streets of Frankton. Since its debut event back in 2008 the ITM Hamilton 400 has become a major success not just for Hamilton but for the whole of New Zealand and it has generated millions of dollars for the City. I am a big V8 Supercars fan and I support the Fords because frankly I hate everything too do with the Holden. It is funny though actually because I used to be a big Holden fan but for some reason at around age 13 I began supporting the Fords, I think it was because I like the underdog in any sport and at that point Holden were very dominant in the sport. All racing fans from New Zealand will know about the number 51 driver, seen as though I do not have permission to mention his name I will not write it in this book but I cannot stand the man. Your going to find it very funny again because I was a fan of this guy but Bathurst 2005 changed all that, I don't like a driver who has a attitude and thinks he is better than everyone else, it may be a little different if the driver actually had a reason to think of himself like that and I don't believe a few race wins amongst other things entitles you to think of yourself in the manner that this man does. None the less he has achieved a lot in the sport of V8 Supercars and he has done wonders for the sport in this country. He will always be known as the most dominant race driver in NZ motorsport history, but there have been a number of very successful motorsport people to come out of this country. Everyone that I know anyway has some sort of connection with sport, either they play it or they have a very healthy interest in it. That is something I would like to talk about if I may for a moment, now Rugby and Rugby League are two very different sports and I hate it when people say League is boring in comparison to Union. In my opinion anyway League is just as hard a game as Union if not harder, I think the six tackle rule is good too because it keeps the game fresh and alive. The Kiwi national league side has been on a roll in recent years after shocking the world by winning the world cup and then a couple of seasons later when they won the four nations trophy, two different tournaments that most League fans did not give the Kiwis a chance of winning. That is the great thing about NZ

Sport, we are always the underdog and we almost all ways defy the odds, take last years Football World Cup for example, no one gave the All Whites a chance to perform well at all but we did and I am very happy about that. Those three games we played are another example of sporting moments that will live through time. In recent years though a major sporting passion of mine has been the WWE, and I will talk about this later on in the book. I cannot remember where the hell I started here, oh yes we were talking about the middle years, lets get back to it then shall we. Well you see those days were very important too me looking back, there are countless memories which I am going to try and share with you now. I have always been fascinated with the locomotive, for those of you who do not know what that word means, it is a word meaning train and in particular the steam engine. Since before I can remember I have been interested in steam trains, and I am lucky that I live where I do because we are near some great railway track and it is very scenic, perfect for taking pictures which is where my next sentence topic will begin. Just quickly, isn't New Zealand a fine country don't you think. Scenery everywhere you look. Thankfully my father had a similar interest in steam trains to and there are countless memories of us chasing the steam train through the King Country district and getting photos of the train going over the viaduct or going into the tunnel on the way to Taumaranui. The railway scenery is some of the best around where I live and I will remember these days for the rest of my life. I can still picture me and dad racing down the road breaking all speed limits whilst trying to catch up with the train, you will be surprised how fast those trains can actually go and people really do not understand the power and majesty behind those awesome trains. Since the mid too late 70s steam trains have been out of commission and replaced by the shitty diesel and electric engines that still run today, people rave about how steam trains ruin the atmosphere because of the smoke and everything but I love them. The sound of the steam engine is the best thing about them I think, and the sight of them on a cold winter's morning just gets me going like nothing else. New Zealand is a particularly lucky country because of the number of keen enthusiasts around the place and there are a number of worldwide respected rail companies that specialise in restoring famous New Zealand steam engines. There are around four different companies in this field around the country and they often run special excursions in the best parts of railway around New Zealand. Many people believe that the best train excursion you can take around this country is the midland line trip that goes through the Southern Alps and the journey goes from Christchurch to Greymouth and return everyday. The trip has become on of the more popular tourist attractions that New Zealand has to offer. My parents went on that train trip back in 1999 and they said the trip offered up one of the most scenic experiences they had ever had the opportunity to experience, I hope you understood that because I sure as hell didn't. My parents were lucky enough to go on this trip in the middle of winter so they got the best experience that the trip can offer with all the snow on the mountains and all that cool stuff. When the steam trains run on that trip it is one of the sights that everyone needs to witness at sometime during there life because I can tell you that you will not only get some great photo shots but you will get to see some of the greatest sights that world train travel has to offer. Usually we would only get a couple of steam excursions going past our way every year and I remember getting so excited at school the week before because I knew that a steam train was coming within days and it drove me wild with excitement, as a kid you always have things to be excited about be it birthdays or other cool events like that, I was a very excitable child and it continues to this day. My favourite steam trains include J1211 and JA 1250 which are in my opinion the most beautiful and well reserved steam engines out of the very few that are still running around the country from time to time today. One of my more favourite train chasing memories was back in 2006 when the good old 'Steam Saturday's" used to run from Auckland down to my hometown of Te Kuiti and then they would spend an hour downtown turning the engine followed by a full service before it was back to Auckland for the return journey, for the few months that this trip ran it was absolute bliss for me. I was loving school at this point and also I began doing something that well is interesting, I began playing cricket whilst watching it on the television. Now when I say this I mean I would sit right on the edge of the coffee table in the lounge and copy what the players on screen did. For example, when the batsmen would swing for the ball on screen I would be sitting on the table swinging my little cricket bat!!!! Or if it was rugby season I would be rolling around on the floor throwing my ball around imagining I was an All Black kicking the winning penalty or scoring the try. At times I would even be tackling an imaginary opponent, I have always had such a widespread imagination. I did this for a few years and I can still remember those days very clearly in my head as I write this. Other memories of these classic years include the days of fishing with dad and going to the beach over Easter. The family on my mums side have been going to Mokou for generations, Mokou is a seaside resort and we have been going there for so many years now and it holds a very special place in my heart for so many reason, when I think of Easter I always think of the beach. There are so many memories from Mokou that I hardly know where to begin, from riding the motorbikes with Uncle all the way to building dams with the sand. Some of the best memories of my life belong at the beach, I remember back in 2003 I spent basically the entire weekend riding the three wheeled motorbikes with uncle Paul or uncle Gary, both have been very good to me over the years and I am very thankful for that. Our family has always been very close especially on my Mums side. It is very easy too say that I have the best Poppa in the whole wide world, Poppa Bob has always been a very big part of my life and I am sure he is the most knowledgeable person I have ever met. The great thing about my Poppa is that you can bring up a topic and before you know it three hours have passed and your still talking about the same thing, and it never gets boring in fact I love it. He has taught me a lot about life over the years and he was especially helpful to me when I made the move from high school too tertiary education and the advise he gave me proved too be invaluable for the first few months at tech where I studied computers for the first year and then the second I studied business. I learnt a lot of life lessons at Wintec. Back to my Poppa Bob. I remember I was at around age 6 maybe, and I was very excited to go to Nana and Poppa's house because of several reasons, but one reason stood out more than any other at that point. My Poppa Bob has got a model train layout in his garage and it is one of the most interesting and well put together things that I have ever seen and it takes me off guard every time I look at it, even too this day it manages to amaze me. This very layout has inspired me and I have my own collection of model trains today, although I will never have the collection that my Poppa owns I am proud of my own model railway. For the middle years of my life I spent a lot of time with model trains be it my own collection or the layout at Poppa Bobs place. I remember one particular weekend where the family and I went too Poppa's house and I could not sleep the night before because I was so excited. Then the next day it was off to Cambridge and I was straight into the garage with Poppa and for the entire afternoon I spent time playing with the model trains, he has a fine collection too I must say. I have no idea where he managed too find all of his model trains but what I learnt a few years later was very interesting, he would go too garage sales with Nana all the time and through that he would find old unused model trains of which he would buy and take them home to fix them, then before you knew it they would be running around on his layout the next time you went too visit. His collection of model trains is staggering, from the famous "big boy" model all the way too the "mallard" it amazes me how he managed to find all these trains which would go for thousands of dollars if they were on the market. Prices of these trains if you want too buy them off the shelf start at around $700 so they are not cheap, and it is awesome that Poppa managed to collect all these wonderful trains. So visits to Nanna and Poppa were very popular with myself over the years and that garage holds a very special place in my heart, after spending a long day in the garage Nanna Bet would have a nice home cooked meal waiting for Poppa and I and she was a great cook. My Nana Bet was another inspiration too me, she was very kind and she was the perfect Nana. When she passed away we were all very devastated and eight years on we still remember the days with her, my last real memory with her was at the beach in Easter of 2003 and I can remember sitting with her watching the road above the valley and we were trying to see if we could spot the campervan of a family member who was on her way too the beach from the south. Very much like Poppa Bob, you could have very long discussions with Nana Bet about topics and time just passed you buy, I remember having a very in depth discussion with her about Coronation Street and the current storylines, that was just before she died and I remember that conversation very well. Sadly she died of a stroke in May of 2003 and it left a whole inside of us that can never be filled but Poppa has done so well since her death and in fact he has not slowed down at all he has remained very active and at 82 he is one of the most active people I know. So my grandparents took up a big part of the middle years of my life, I loved every moment spent doing things with them and it sucks because at the time of writing this book I only have one grandparent left and that is Poppa Bob. My dad has been working in the roading management sector for well over 20 years now and he is one of the most respected men in the industry and he has a wealth of knowledge, so much of that he currently is training cadets at work to hopefully do what he does in the future. When I was little I would go out with dad to work all the time and usually I would end up in the trucks with guys who worked with dad while he would be back at the job site inspecting all the work that was being done and making sure it was up too standard. Im what about age 8 now and things are going along very well, a year or so earlier I was moved from Te Kuiti Primary School to Pukenui School just across town. The reason for this was because a particular student was physically bullying me, for example I was in a manual wheelchair at this point and this person would come up behind me and push the chair towards the stairs, which would scare me no end. To this day it still kind of scares me and I try and avoid being anywhere near stairs if I can help it. I was moved from the school for this reason and also because my parents were disgusted with how the bullying was dealt with or the lack of, mum and dad were not prepared to keep me in the school with this going on, bullying is one thing but physically intimidating others that cannot fight back is another. I was not the only student that this person bullied, I know for a fact that he went after two other people who were friends of mine. I will talk about bullying a little later on in this book. At age 9 I attended my first ever MDN Camp in Auckland, MDN is short for the Muscular Dystrophy Northern branch and we had our first ever camp at Buckland's Beach in Auckland way back in 2001. It was at this camp that I met a few life long friends including my best friend Brooke who is also in a wheelchair and he has Duchene Muscular Dystrophy. I love Brooke and we are very close, I remember the first time I ever saw him and I will never forget it. Brooke has always been a very quiet person and still too this day it takes a bloody miracle too get a rise out of the block, but he is my best mate. Like most friends we have had our share of disagreements in the past but I think that deep down we both know how much we need each other and I also think that the fact we are both disabled is the reason why we are so close, we both know what the other is going through and there is something about that which comforts the both of us in a way that I cannot really describe if I am honest. I had met Brooke a couple of times earlier before the camp but I really got to know him over the course of the week long camp up in Auckland, we spent most of the day playing wheelchair hockey together when we were not going on outings,

I remember the day when we went to the Sky Tower and his mum nearly died of shock when you go up in the lift and all of a sudden the wall in front of the lift window disappears and out of nowhere a window appears and your way above ground level, I am sure it would be a shock for anyone who had not been up the tower before. Since 2001 we have had a few camps for all us kids and we have had lots of fun over the years. Camps are really special for kids who have a physical condition and it is also comforting for the parents, sometimes when you live this life you feel like you alone and that no one else is going through what you are. When you see other people who not only have the same condition as yourself but have been through or are currently going through the almost exact same thing that your going through yourself, that is a huge help when you can talk to people in the same position that you are. I think that may be the reason why Brooke and me are so close, we have this feeling of understanding between us. One of the more serious but very crucial stages of the middle years took place at around age 7 when I began using what it called a standing frame; a standing frame is like this big steel robot like piece of equipment. It has wheels at the bottom so you can move around in it, basically I would be lifted into this standing frame and from a sitting position this machine stands you upright. I would stand upright in this standing frame for an hour once or twice a day for about 3 years. It would be very tiring for me but once again it was something that had to be done, as it was crucial for my physical development. At age 7 my Mum got a part time job looking after a young girl, Claudia is like a sister too me and I love her very much. We spent everyday together for around 4 years, as Mum would look after her while Claudia's mum would be at work here in Te Kuiti. It seems like only yesterday, but Claudia is now 14 years old and she has grown up so much. It is another one of those friendships that will last forever. Pukenui School was now my new school, and well I am not going to say it was the ideal setup for me again met some life long friends there. At age nine was when something that would become almost the norm for me for the next ten years or so was the bullying and it came to a beginning at Pukenui School, although I had been bullied back at Te Kuiti Primary, it was at the new school a couple of years later that the mental and physical trauma really began for me. My dad has always been very keen into the sport of fishing, I really think that dad is the most constant of fisherman and he will never give up the opportunity to get on the boat and spend hours sitting down holding onto a fishing rod waiting for a bite. I have never really understood the sport of fishing, it is too slow for me. I used to go white baiting with dad when it was the correct season and I have also been fishing with him a few times. I remember as a child I would get super excited when the fish was smoked, have you ever had smoked fish??? The smell of it is so good and I can tell you there is nothing like the taste of smocked fish. We used to have a workmate of dads smoke our fish but sadly he is no longer with us on this earth, now my cousin Alex does it. Actually too this day I still love the show, but when I was younger I was obsessed with Thomas The Tank Engine and I would ever always be watching the show or playing with my little Thomas Trains that mum and dad would always buy me. I love that show and it is one of the best kid shows out there, it is better than some of the rubbish that you seen on the box these days. Things were simple back in the day weren't they. Things were rolling along for my family and me at this stage, personally I was very happy and determined child and I knew very well what I wanted from the future. I was a normal child and the fact that I was disabled had not even registered in my mind because I was in such a good home I felt like I could achieve anything despite being in a difficult situation in regards to my health and physical ability. Interesting times were a head for my family and me however; I was about to go through an amazingly risky but crucial operation that would change not just my life but all of our lives forever.

Chapter 4: Learning To Live Again

I am twelve years of age now and it has been one of the best childhoods I think a kid could possibly ask for, but things were about to change for us all. Life is very precious these days and no one knows that more than myself. With my disability Spinal Muscular Dystrophy physical movement is limited and every year I have a major assessment to see where I am at, and what possibly could be done too try and help me out. One of the big shall we say symptoms of my disability is that my spine curves; basically when you look at my spine is looks like your looking at a S shape. Back when I was nine years old I had an appointment with a surgeon too determine wether or not I would need to have major spinal surgery to try and potentially straighten my back. So it was off too Auckland for the appointment where I had to go through major tests to see if my young body would be able to cope with the magnitude of the operation, I remember being very scared looking at all the tests I had too go through. It is not an easy thing to deal with. So after a morning of various tests it was time for the appointment and after carful consideration from the surgeon involved he decided that it was too risky for me to undergo a operation that is this risky. In a way it was a big relief for my parents, as I did not have to have the operation, for now anyway. I guess your all wondering what this operation involves??? Well let me try and break it down right here for you all. The point of this surgery is to try and straighten the spine, as my back was curving at a very bad angle. What the doctor wanted was to insert a steel rod into the spine and then screw it into the bone, what would happen once this rod was placed into my back as I would grow the rod would force the spine to straighten. It is known as one of the most invasive and risky operations on record and it was made clear too my parents that I may not make it through, the chances of dying during the surgery are minimum but still the risk is there. However the first time we had an appointment about this surgery we were told by the doctor that the risks of not pulling through outweighed the possibility of a full recovery. In a way we were very relieved that we did not have to go through this major change, well for the time being anyhow. Many doctors around the world do this operation everyday, and I have seen and met five of them over the years. I was relived that I did not have to have surgery but I have to admit back at that age I did not really understand the whole thing. I remember that I got presents out of the initial appointment though as reward for going through all the major tests my young body had to have to try and determine what to do. At this stage it was looking like I would never have the operation because the initial doctor that we saw did not think that I would make it through, but often you find that different doctors have different ways of testing and looking at things. So it was back to the normal everyday life that we live, school, work and everything else living in great harmony. Then three years later we met a man named Hamish and he was very keen on getting me to have the spinal surgery that would improve my health, but again the risk was there. It was the year 2003 now and I was a lot more grown up and had a fair idea about life and my disability so I was very nervous and anxious about the prospects of major surgery. I remember talking to some friends of mine who were also in wheelchairs and had been through this operation, but I think they did not give me the full story because if they did I would probably refuse the surgery it is that bad in reality. We got a phone call from Hamish and he wanted to see us as soon as possible to discuss things, so before I knew it we were off to Hamilton for an appointment and tests. The first thing that we had to do was get me an X Ray and that went very well and then it was time to sit and wait for our appointment to begin. Have you ever had an outpatient's appointment at Waikato Hospital? Well if you have not I can tell you that the people are never on time!!!! However they are very busy so I am sure they have their reasons. Over the years I have dealt with many, many doctors and surgeons and they are all very good people and they know there stuff, I have the most respect for these people because in my opinion they are some of the world's great people and they deserve all the recognition that they get. Without them I would not be here today there is no doubting that. So once we got into the meeting with Hamish the first words out of his mouth were that he wanted to go ahead with spinal surgery, I was very upset when he told me this. I was upset because it is a very scary thing and I knew that it would be life changing for me and my family, I felt really sorry for Hamish because it must be a very difficult thing to tell a family especially with a operation of this magnitude. I remember asking Hamish if I was going to die, a random yet very important question it felt to me at the time. Hamish then went on to tell us all about the mechanics of the operation and he gave us a date, mid year 2004 which was about 6 months away. I was scared but understood why I needed to have the surgery, the reason why I needed this done was too try and straighten the spine. When the spine starts to curve like mine was it begins to push itself down on the lungs therefore making it very difficult to breathe as I would grow. My surgeon wanted to get on top of this before it became a big issue. So we left the appointment with mixed feelings and we were also comfortable in the knowledge that we had a wee while to get prepared for this surgery as it was six months away. I would be having the surgery in Starship Children's Hospital in Auckland, I had never been here for an operation so that made me a little anxious. I am very much a person that likes to know how things are going to be before I do them, and I like to know every aspect down to the finest of details, some people may call this obsessive but I think its good if you know what your going to get into, obsessive? You can be the judge. The six months managed to pass very quickly, during this time I was mostly at school and we had the odd family occasion to attend plus I managed to get to the MDN Camp which was held that year at Totara Springs in Matamata. A couple of weeks before the time I was due to have the surgery we got a phone call from the surgical team and they told us that they would need to put off the operation for a couple of months due to forces out of there control, you know how it is someone gets drunk and has an accident and requires a bed therefore taking my bed at the hospital, that is one of the most annoying and frustrating things I have found with the health system in this country, the good people's beds keep getting taken by a person who has injured themselves due to there lack of self control when it comes to alcohol. The news that my surgery had been delayed stuffed me up in the head a little bit, because by this time I had got prepared for the operation mentally and that is the biggest thing you have to do pre surgery and then when you think you have got your head around everything someone stuffs everything up. It is not that big of a deal looking back but it did affect the mental preparation of what was going to be a major, life changing operation. So the surgery was put off until November of 2004 and once again the time between when the operation was originally going to take place to the new date managed to fly by very quickly and before I knew it we were off to Auckland for the pre surgery tests. This time it was a little different however because the test that I was going to have were very in depth and well to be honest they were very scary. The first of which is the breathing test, this involved me getting into a capsule like piece of equipment where they have to close the door and go into another room and I breathe into the machine for as long as possible before you get tired, whilst this is happening the breathing results come up on there computer and they can then determine various different factors for during the operation. Then it was off for the heart test and that is where the person sticks a whole lot of electrodes to your chest and arms to test your heart strength, this is the most major test because if your heart is not strong enough to survive a operation that can last anywhere between six to twelve hours. Yes people this was a major operation because it takes almost an entire day to complete which is why the risks that I was talking about before are so high and it is also why these tests I was having were so important and I had no choice but to go through them. Believe me if I could have got out of them I would have done so. Oddly the worst test I had was the blood test, I can hear you laughing right now but there is something about needles and injections that just makes my skin crawl. Then after all these tests it was time for a sit down with Hamish and he talked us through the surgery and answered all the questions we were having. It had been a very long day and we were left feeling very happy but still at the same time very anxious and nervous about the week ahead, it was Friday at this point and the surgery was going to take place the following Tuesday in the morning. So we had the weekend to ourselves, and interestingly enough this was one of the more memorable weekends during my life. We spent the weekend shopping and I remember being spoilt rotten, we saw a whole lot of family and friends and it was just such a great weekend. As I said the operation was scheduled for the Tuesday and we were going to leave for Auckland on the Monday. I remember sitting up the back of our section on the Monday whilst my parents were packing up the house and thinking about my life and everything I had been through up until this point. I remember being very worried and wondering if this may be the last day I ever spend at my own house, the risk of death was never there really, but you just cannot help feeling very anxious and nervous. It sounds a little harsh towards my parents, but there was nothing they could really say to make me feel any better about the operation. So it was off to Auckland in the car and it was a lovely summer's day outside. When we got to the hospital it was time for a walk around and various other things. Then a quick shower and off to bed. Mum stayed with me in my room and dad went to what's called the Ronald McDonald House which is a special house in the hospital for the family members of a kid who is have major surgery, the house has cooking facilities and lovely rooms. It is a very big comfort for families because they do not need to worry about where there going to stay for the often long periods of time that their child may be in hospital for. So we said goodnight to dad and I went to bed. I did not sleep too much the night before my surgery and I doubt if my parents did either as we were all nervous and worried. So the night was a very long one but before we knew it, it was morning and the day had come. I was not allowed to drink or eat anything on the morning of the surgery, Hamish made a special trip to come and see me before he went to prepare for the operation. He assured us that everything would be fine and I would be in recovery before I knew it. I really admire Hamish, not many surgeons would make the effort to come and see their patient just minutes before a major operation like this one. Then a lady came in with a glass full of this white, drink sort of thing which I had to swallow. You can probably imagine what this stuff is. As soon as I had swallowed this drink, I began feeling very odd and floaty. From what I can remember I literally felt like I was flying around the room, it is such a great feeling and I imagine it gives you more of a buzz than any illegal drug can offer you, I cannot stand illicit drugs and I think you have to be a pretty low human being to even consider going there to be honest. I remember my dad talking to me and it got more distant and more distant as the minutes went on and I began to drift in and out of consciousness and the last real memory I have before the surgery was seeing the lift doors close as we were on our way down to the operating room. The drugs that the people gave me were amongst the most powerful that can be given to a patient who is about to undergo major surgery. Mum and dad got very emotional when I was put to sleep and they saw the seriousness of the situation, basically once I was out they had to put me inside of the bed thing face down, the bed was like a table that could be jacked up off the floor. When I was asleep there were people working on my back and people underneath the table monitoring my breathing and my heart rate, all that very important stuff. The fact that mum and dad had to put my life in the hands of other people was extremely difficult for them and they got quite upset at the start when I was first put too sleep. It would become on of the longest days of their life, the surgery lasted 12 hours. I kid you not, they said it would take around 9 hours to complete the surgery but it took a lot longer than they expected. My parents ran into Hamish during the surgery while he was on break and he assured them that everything was going ok and I would be back to recovery in no time. Again, the surgery sees the team of surgeons place two steel rods in my back and then once they are in place they screw then into the bone of the spine using various power tools. Then it was time for me to be woken up, I can remember how this went in heaps of detail. I remember having a dream about Thomas The Tank Engine, and then hearing "Michael can you hear me" slowly getting louder and louder, then suddenly a light appeared and boy it was bright. I then noticed that around twenty people were standing around me all asking me various things at once, it is a very daunting experience and you don't quite know what is going on. To be honest I was not in too much pain when I first woke up from the operation, my head just felt very heavy and there was noises of machines all around me. I was then moved into the intensive care unit, and here is where I quickly descended into hell at a very rapid pace. My parents were not aloud to see me for the first couple of hours post surgery for obvious reasons. Once I was in intensive care and all setup was when mum and dad, and my sister Jenna came to see me. I cannot remember too much of this, all I really remember from the first night spent in intensive care was the intense pain I felt. It was the single longest night of my life, drifting in and out of sleep and crying pretty much the entire time I was awake. Mum and dad were told to come back in the morning and I was not happy about that, you don't really understand all that much when your just hours out of major surgery. You don't really care about any bloody thing because all you want is for the pain to go away, I would have given anything for that. The next morning when I woke up was when the pain and hell really began, I realised that something had happened here that I was not expecting, and that was the massive amount of pain that I began feeling. Lets see if I can try and paint a picture here for you. I was just hours out of major surgery and I was hooked up to all sorts of computers and needles, I could not move and inch and my back felt like it had been taken too with a chainsaw. I no longer had any bladder control and was relying on a cafitor, which is the single most painful part of the entire experience. The morning after the surgery was spent unhooking my body from all these machines as they were preparing to move me back to the ward. The nurse had to pull out all the needles that were attached to my body whilst I was screaming in pain. Mum and dad said that when they first saw me after the surgery they could not recognise me, I had lost over 20KG during the operation and I had major welt marks on my stomach and chest as I had been lying face down for twelve hours. Once I was moved out of intensive care I would be under 24 hour observation and one of the surgeons was at my beside for the next couple of days along with mum and dad of course. I cannot describe how painful and horrible the next couple of weeks would become, I was literally in hell. I did not get much sleep and it would take hours to try and get me comfortable, and when they managed to do so it would be time for me to go and have an X Ray which would involve me being moved onto another bed causing even more intense pain. I had to have X Rays every day, sometimes more than once. During this time it was very hard on all of us, I was not eating and due to the drugs I was on I was a very angry young man, no one could get anything right no matter what they did. There were some quite funny moments along the way as well, I remember refusing to eat for days and when Jenna went to get McDonalds suddenly I was hungry and ended up eating her entire meal much to her surprise. From there I began to eat again, and things were starting to pick up slowly. However we had another major worry at this point, during my stay at the hospital mum got very sick and she ended up in hospital as well!!!! She got some weird illness that was stress related, who could blame her considering what she had seen her son go through in recent times. Were we all very stressed at this point. Mum was making steady process but we were all very worried about her. The fact that I no longer had bladder control really messed with me, has anyone reading this ever had to use a cafitor??? Well you will know what it is like. One time when we went to lift me the cord got caught up on the bed and therefore the cafitor go ripped out of my willy causing the most intense pain I think a man could ever go through. Then it had to be put back in which was even worse. We are about two weeks post surgery now and it was time to go home, however due to my condition I was going to be transferred back to Te Kuiti and stay at the hospital here. I loved it!!!! As mum was a nurse there for 25 years I got the royal treatment and it really helped me during my recovery, during my days at Te Kuiti hospital I would drive around the carparks in my wheelchair and whilst I was doing this it was building up the strength in my back. Then I went home for the weekend, and it was here when it all went peer shaped. I was getting into bed one night and when dad rolled me over he noticed some fluid like stuff on his hands. Then he had a look at my back and saw that it had broken up, there was literally a hole in my back where the scar was and it was leaking a tone of fluid. So quickly he rang the hospital and someone came around to patch it up. Then after a very anxious next couple of days, we were told the worst possible news that we could have wanted. I was going to have to go back to hospital, for more surgery. We were all very upset and had just about reached the end of our rope by this point, I remember bursting into tears when we got the news. So we went up to Waikato Hospital the next day for a meeting to try and see what could be done, within minutes my surgeon Hamish was on the phone demanding that they transfer us back to Auckland right away. So we headed up there and that night the entire surgical team came to look at my back and it was decided that I would undergo surgery the next day to try and clear out the injection. My back had become infected, this is a common occurrence when there is a steel item inside the human body and sadly it is just one of those things. I was very unhappy at this point. I went for the surgery the next day and it only lasted for a couple of hours, the problem has been partly solved but I would go on to have another surgery. It was sheer luck that they managed to discover yet another injection in my back during the operation, these surgeries were not anywhere as near as bad as the big one a month earlier. After these two minor operations things began to pick up and before I knew it we were back in Te Kuiti and I was back with my friends at the hospital. The nurses here were all mums friends, they were so nice. They would make me a whole range of great meals if I did not like the hospital food which was pretty much all the time. It was decided that I would need 6 hourly drug treatment, and I was steering down the barrel of staying in hospital for the next 6 months. Then step up mum!!!!! As you all know she is a former nurse and she decided that rather than stay in hospital for six months I would go home and she would do my treatment every six hours for the foreseeable future. It just makes me love her even more, for her to step up like this at a time when I was at my lowest speaks her character, for the next couple of months she would be treating me every six hours with the IV drugs, lets not forget that she was very sick herself at this point too. What a great mum, she is the best woman I know and I love and thank her very much. There was quite a lot of small things that I did when in the recover stage and they would prove to be very crucial. Dad and I would take long walks around the hospital, its seems pretty simple but the more I drove around in my wheelchair the more strong my back got and the more confident I got about wandering around. Often dad would be very tough on me, because you sometimes have to be. I was not the most co operative person in the world when I was in hospital, especially when it came to eating. Due to the surgery I lost the ability to feed myself and after weeks of having someone do it for me dad decided one night that I needed to at least give it a go, I was not happy about this. A big thing dad taught me during this time was that with a little perseverance and confidence you can regain some strength. My dad is very much a get on with it type of guy, in my opinion that is the best way to be especially these days. When I was staying in Te Kuiti hospital in the later stages of recovery I would go home with dad on the weekends and in a way it was a real bonding experience for the both of us, dad was very caring about me. Usually dad is a very tough and not to much of an emotional type of guy, but when things get difficult he is very caring. He has a heart that is bigger than anyone I know, he is the true definition of a man and that is someone who is there for his family all the time. He works very hard to look after us and I admire him for that, I wish kids these days had the same values that mum and dad have taught me. Your parents are the most important people in our lives and we should always appreciate them. It was early December at this point and I did need to stay in Te Kuiti hospital for a wee while longer for observation, the doctors just wanted to make sure my body was ok. I ended up being discharged from hospital on the 23rd of December 2004, just two days before Christmas. Lady luck was back in my corner with the timing. When we got home and I got the chance to sleep in my own bed once again, we all felt like things were getting back to normal and there is something about that which is very comforting. I remember going back to the back of our section on Christmas Eve to think and reflect, just like I had done the day before my surgery a couple of months earlier. It brings a tear to my eyes at times when you think about it, it was Christmas Eve and the sun was out. In just two months my life had changed almost completely, I had to learn how to live again and I mean that very seriously. If there is something that I love more than anything else on this planet it is Christmas, there is nothing that compares to that time of year. I am not going to lie, there were times lying in that hospital bed up in Auckland when I wondered if I was going to see another Christmas, at times I just wanted to die to get away from the pain. Through it all the surgery was a great success and I now could breathe freely again, my spine was already a lot straighter. I thank Hamish for taking a risk and giving me the surgery because without it I would not be sitting here writing this book today, I probably would have been dead a long time ago if not for Hamish. I now am very healthy, not a lot of people with this disability can say they went through this surgery and came out with a better way of like than they did before. I had been through the mill, and my life had changed for the better.

Chapter 5: The Years At School

Life as we all know can be great at times and it can be equally as bad sometimes. I have been too three schools in my lifetime which compared to a lot of other kids in this country is not many, I know some people that have been moved from school to school and are very much used to being "the new kid" which must be difficult. Interestingly enough when I went to the new schools I always fitted into place quite nicely and managed to find friends very easily. I remember when I moved from Te Kuiti Primary School over to Pukenui School, the first day at the new school I ran into an old friend from pre school and he went on to become one of my best mates of all time. I had a very interesting schooling life, at times it was great and others it was downright horrible. We will get onto that a little later but for now I want to talk about the importance of school if I may. Without a shadow of a doubt school is one of the most important things in life and it is crucial for your development, we all learn a lot during our time at school and all the important things like maths, english and all that good stuff is covered. One of the big things that annoys these days is when people drop put of school thinking they know what they are doing, when in fact they really have no idea and once you have left that is it the game is over. The trend today seems to be drop out of school and go get a job at the local supermarket of something, not everyone does this but if you look at the stats it is becoming more and more frequent which concerns me for several reasons, one of which is where the education system is going to be in lets say ten years time. There are some students who take there schooling very seriously and there are others who simply don't give two cares about it, the signs of a student being very motivated or unmotivated are very clear right from the outset in the early years of their education. I was always pretty successful inside the classroom, especially during the early years. Usually when you first begin school you do things like drawing or learning the alphabet, I was good at both of these things. I remember trying to learn the times table, I was doing fine until we got up to 12, it took me ages to try and learn that. My parents were good and they helped me a lot, they even put up the times table on the wall of the toilet so I could practice while doing the business. After that it did not take me very long for me to learn my times table and before I knew it I was passing all my maths tests. This is going to be a very long chapter so bear with me readers because there is a lot that I need to cover here. So shall we start with primary school? I think that would be a good place to start. At age 5 I began primary school like most other children and I was very excited and managed to make friends in no time, actually I have always had no problem talking to people so that is a bonus for me. I was at Te Kuiti Primary at this time and I spent most of my school days working in class and playing with the gutter boards during lunch hour, all I needed was a ball and something to throw it against and I was set most of the time. You often find that when your young it is the simple things that keep you entertained the most and I was no exception, from age 5 till age 9 I spent most of my spare time outside playing cricket or rugby, whatever I could manage that was what I would do, I wish I could still do that these days but physically things have changed. I remember one special lunchtime at Te Kuiti Primary when me and my mates decided to have a game of rugby and I was right up for it, I got the teacher aid to lift me out of my wheelchair and onto the field at school so I could play. I lasted one tackle and the ball was stripped out of my hands within a few seconds but I had a blast none the less. It was during this lunch hour when I noticed something about my disability for the first time, I noticed that I was not as strong as the other kids and I did not know why, but I just shrugged it off and continued to play trying my very best in every situation. One of the most special moments of my life occurred during my time at Te Kuiti Primary School, it was when the royal variety bash came to town. The royal variety bash is an organisation that travels the country raising funds for various charities, and when they came to Te Kuiti that day I was the special someone receiving the royal treatment. As I am writing about this it is making me feel very happy just remembering that day, I met tons of celebrities and was on TV, amongst other things me and the school received a big check for me and the special needs department in the school. I still have the video of that day lying around the house somewhere. I remember spending a lot of time with the crew from a famous TV program in NZ, the camera just followed me and my family around all day. There is a famous classic fire engine that I got to ride around in with my sister as well, it was such a good day for me and I remember it well. It is one of those memories that will never leave me. Often during life when you are disabled you find that certain charities often take an interest in you and it is good because some disabled people don't have the quality of life that I have had, it makes me happy to know that these charities do all they can to ensure a child can be out of pain, if only for a minute, its still worth it. Things at Te Kuiti Primary School were going along quite fine at this point and I had made a lot of friends in no time at all, I was very happy and was achieving very well in the classroom. It was around this time that I began using the standing frame and often I would use it during school when I would be in class doing my work. All the other kids were very interested in the standing frame and the teacher aid and I would always be getting asked various things about the machine. My friends would say things like "how come your able to stand now" and "why can't you stand all the time" all very cute and honest questions that a youngster would ask. Back during these days I was always very confident in myself and the disability. I had a lot of fun during lunch hours at Te Kuiti Primary, one day I had a crazy idea and decided to join the school tug of war team for something else to do during lunch hour. Mum and dad were very happy that I joined and despite my lack of strength I still gave it the best shot possible. I remember during one tug or war I was right at the back of the line and the force of the pull almost pulled me out of my wheelchair, it gave me a hell of a shock but I loved that game very time I played it. So things were going very well and I was doing very well at school, but then something began to happen to me that would become a very common trend at school as the years went on. Every couple of days another young man in the school, he was a year older than me and he felt it would be funny to begin bullying me whenever he saw me, at first he only did it a few times but it began happening more and more often too the point where he began physically intimidating me. I was in a manual wheelchair at this point, this guy would come up behind me and push the wheelchair towards the stairs with me being totally defenceless and unable to stop him from doing it. I would love to name everyone who bullied me throughout my life but sadly I do not have permission to use their names in this book due to copyright reasons. Below is a short list of bullies who will feature a lot during this chapter.

- Bully A (Te Kuiti Primary School Age 7)
- Bully B (Pukenui School & Te Kuiti High School Age 9 – 16)

They are two of the bullies who were the worst during the school years. So bully A amongst other things would push me towards the stairs, it is only pure luck in my case that every time he would do this someone would be there to grab me just before I was about to tumble down the stairs. During class bulla A would punch me and steal my equipment thinking it was such a big joke. I was not the only person that bully A gave a hard time too, I remember walking into class one day and seeing bully A pin one of my friends up onto the wall and punching him, a bully is nothing but a gutless wonder. So once mum and dad found out about this guy, naturally they went straight to the principle of the school to complain and try and sort this problem out. It was here that something even more mind boggling happened, the principle told my parents that I bring it on all myself!!! Can you believe that? She actually said to my mother that "I have looked into this, and it appears that mike brings all this bullying on himself" and I cannot believe for a second that it was true. So basically I was accused of provoking bully A into pushing me down the stairs? Why in gods name would I do that? Some people who call themselves professional really amaze me at times. My mum was very upset about this to the point when she was in tears at the principle's office because she was worried for me and she did not know what to do about the situation without making the backlash worse for her son. I remember leaving the classroom one day with my teacher aid to go to the toilet and seeing mum there talking to the principle and she had tears in her eyes, as I was only seven years of age it did not really register with me but I still wondered why my mum was upset. When we would be doing our work in the classroom bully A would throw things at me, mainly directed at my head. The teacher never seemed to want to do anything about the situation which gave bully A free range to do whatever he wanted to in the classroom without any consequence which sort of baffles me. Mum and dad did not back down however and wanted a solution to this problem so they continued to go and see the principle of the school, all she said to them was that I bring on bullying myself, I will say right now I do not bring it on myself and I was very scared of this guy. When your that young and your being bullied you don't really notice and first, but I can tell you I sure noticed it when my wheelchair was heading towards the steps. My parents were now faced with a big problem and they could not talk anyone at Te Kuiti Primary School that actually cared enough to try and sort this problem out, all they got told from the principle was either "Mike brings it on himself" and "there is nothing I can do about this" which is two comments that really bug me when I think about it, bullying is a world wide issue and at least in NZ it can be a major issue trying to stop it. People use all sorts of excuses as to why they bully but I don't believe nor feel sorry for any bully on this planet. One day at school bully A punched me in the chest quickly followed by a punch to the rips when I told him to leave me alone, like a gutless bully does he did it when no one else was around when I was pushing my self in the wheelchair from the toilets back into the classroom, I have no idea why he was even out of the class to begin with because he was not in the toilet block. When he punched me a started to cry, the pain was unbelievable and when the teacher came to look for me I was too scared to tell her what happened because of fear that bully A would come after me again. For a little while there my parents were wondering what they could do about the whole situation, the thought of taking it further was a good idea but at the same time the process of dealing with the board of trustees would take a lot of time therefore increasing the amount of potential bullying from this kid. When my parents found out about the physical bullying they were angry and upset, one day when my mum was picking me up from school she got into a conversation with my teacher aid about the bullying and she suggested that it was time for me to be pulled out of the school. The teacher aid told mum that it was pointless trying to talk to the principle and management because they simply did not want to know anything about students being bullied and all they wanted to do was focus on the educational part of the school, so it then looked like we had no choice. Mum and dad made the decision to pull me out of Te Kuiti Primary School at the end of the term and it was a decision we were all happy with and now all we had to do was try and find me a new school to move too. In Te Kuiti there are four main primary schools so we decided to have a good look around during the holidays. After having a good look around we decided that I would move to Pukenui School down on King Street, about a ten minute walk from my house. Going to this new school presented another slight problem however, I had just made the move from using a manual wheelchair over to a power wheelchair that would no longer fit in the car and we did not have a van at this point. From my house the school was located around eight streets away and it became clear that I would need to begin driving my wheelchair to and from my new school everyday which made us all a little bit nervous, mainly due to access and other key issues. My first power wheelchair marked a great point in my life, let me try and explain how these things work. Basically it is very similar to a car as in they are not the easiest things to drive if you have never done it before. Just like a car, the power wheelchairs have gears and various speeds, it took me a few months to master the art of driving my chair around the house and the fact that I was driving to school everyday meant I had a lot of opportunities for practise. Wheelchairs run on battery and depending on what type of wheelchair you have battery sizes will vary, this is all decided during the big assessments you have prior to getting a new wheelchair. Moving to a power wheelchair gave me a whole lot of new opportunities for independence, the fact that I could walk to school every day like all the other kids was really cool. For the next four years I would drive myself down the road to school, in the hot summers and the freezing cold winters I got very used to the streets leading from the house to Pukenui School. My early time at Pukenui School was very good for the first few months, I was lucky because my best mate from pre school went to Pukenui School and we hit it off right away on my first day at my new school, I was in room 7 and my teacher was pretty cool and very on to it. The first couple of years here flew by very quickly, during this time I was involved in the school production and I joined the music class for a year or so. Most of the lunchtimes were spent playing cricket on the concrete block with all my friends, I remember one particular game I scored over 100 runs, the rules were slightly different however because every hit counted as a run. Those lunch games were amongst some of the happiest moments of my schooling life, I have always loved my sport and back in the day I would do everything I could to try and join in and play. I joined the school cricket team in 2000 and I managed to play a couple of games but I did not do very well, I am thankful that they made it so I could join in despite the circumstances. I would be around 11 years old now and this was when things began to change slightly for me in more ways than one. My disability was starting to take a more powerful and obvious effect on my life, I was beginning to lose a lot of strength and things that I could do easily before I was now noticing that I either struggled or could not do at all anymore. When this happens it is a real blow to you mentally, and I being such a young age was angry and confused at the same time. I found that I could no longer lift my hand up in class anymore when I needed the teacher and also reaching things became a lot harder when before I had no trouble at all, this is something that all us kids with muscle conditions go through at some point and it is a very tough pill to swallow, you know that your different from most other kids but you don't really understand why whilst at the same time know all the information about the disability. I knew about why I was in a wheelchair and what the disability was all about but nothing really major had happened that would cause me to notice that things were not quite right. Dealing with that is not a easy to thing to do but it was made much easier for me because mum and dad were so supportive of me and especially mum, I could talk to her about anything at anytime and we have had some great conversations, she always manages to cheer me up when I am feeling upset or angry about various situations that arise during life, she is my best friend and you can always talk to her about things if you need advise. My parent and child relationship is very important and I have been blessed with two great role models and very caring parents. The year 2003 proved to be very difficult for one reason and one reason only, let me introduce to you all bully B who I met at Pukenui School, amazingly I used to call him a friend back in the day but when he turned on me he did in the worst possible way. Bully B was a vindictive and cunning bully right throughout the seven years that I knew and him and he very much fits the name bully in every way you can imagine, I thought the bullying from bully A back at Te Kuiti Primary School was bad but that guy was no where near as cunning and smart at being a bully that bully B was, bully B was a tactical son of a bitch and he just knew how to make his bullying happen without anyone noticing. Readers please bear with me because this is going to cover a very rough phase of my life, which lasted over six years. Bully B was as I said a friend of mine until one day he just began bullying me and it was bad, real bad. First he began making fun of me and then it took a more sinister turn when he started to call me the worst names imaginable, I remember being so upset and confused on almost an every day basis due this guy. When you talk about bullies you can think of many different aspects, some people bully physically and others bully mentally but it is safe to say that the mental bullying can at time be worse and cause untold grieve on a person, you read and hear all sorts of accounts or stories of how people have been bullied so much to the point where they loss all control and either do something terrible or commit suicide, that's how bad bullying can get these days. I was bullied by bully B for around six years and in that time he caused a lot of pain for me and my family. Bully B would call me names like retard, handicap and a whole lot more, during one lunch hour in front of all my friends he called me a charity case because in his view everyone who is disabled gets help from the government and the tax payer, he said to me once that "why should people help second class retard citizens like you". I remember how I felt when he said that to me and it was a very horrible feeling and I wanted nothing more than to punch him in the face but I was very scared of him as well and he knew it before I did, he knew that I had no come back for what he was doing and he took pride in physically intimidating me day in day out. There was a very important and somewhat difficult aspect when it came to me and bully B as well, and it was that we both had several mutual friends which made me even more scared of him because I did not want to involve my friends out of fear that he would start either bullying them or getting them to bully me as well. As the years rolled past bully B managed to ruin some very good friendships I had and before I knew it he had a whole gang of people on my case and it began to get physical before to long, one day he had me surrounded and I could not get away, when I tried to get out of the circle they had formed around me bully B punched me in the jaw and when I screamed out for help he then punched me in the stomach. This all happened and no one else seemed to see it nor give me a hand, after he had punched me in the stomach I could not speak and quickly began finding it difficult to breathe and once the group had all had their punch at me I was left crying all alone behind the library. For the rest of the day I was in a lot of pain but I knew that if I said anything to a teacher I would be given a second dose of the treatment I had just received earlier, so I finished my day at school and drove myself home and as soon as I saw mum I burst into tears when she asked where I had got the marks on my face from. As soon as I told her what had happened she was on the phone to the school and scheduled a meeting with the principle for first thing the next morning. So after a relatively sleepless night mum and I were off to the school for the meeting, as soon as we pulled up and got out of the gate bully B was right there ready to have a go but when he saw mum he soon changed his tune, but you could see in his eyes that he would be after me as soon as mum was not there, it was decided that I would go to class while mum had a conversation with the principle. I was waiting to be called into the office but I never was, during the morning interval I saw mum was still in the office so I stayed near by to make sure that bully B stayed away from me because like the gutless bully he was, he never bullied me when a member of authority was around. Then mum came out of the principles office she was clearly not happy and she told me that I would be going to see the principle after morning break, the principle told mum that she will deal with this issue and to go home and not worry, mum was in two minds at this point because on the one hand she wanted me to stay at school because of my education but at the same time she was worried for my welfare and I don't think she was convinced with what the principle had to say to be honest, it must be very hard for a parent when their child is being bullied especially if the school does not impress when you try and deal with the issue the right way. We had been through this whole thing before and we knew that the system does not always do what it claims to. So after morning break I was called into the office and bully B was already there and had been crying by the looks of things but I did not care, it is time he cried for once because I had been doing a lot of this lately, the first thing that came out of the principles mouth was that she wanted this "nonsense" to stop, as if I actually wanted this to happen in the first place. The principle then growled at me for getting mum involved and she said that I should have told someone about it sooner, clearly the principle did not want her "good" little school getting a bad reputation. So me and bully B were made to shake hands and be good little boys and I was consumed with anger at this point because for the majority of the meeting I was the one being yelled at, god forbid I tell my mother that I am being bullied because it may just give the school a bad look. So after the meeting it was back to class and within minutes bully B was on my case once again, so began another years worth of physical and mental bullying. One day I decided to make an appointment to see the principle myself and when I was in there we got into a very heated discussion and I got very upset, when I began to cry the principle got even more angry at me and she told me that I shouldn't go crying to my mother whenever I get bullied, when I asked her why not she said "because bullying happens Michael" and "I need to get used to being bullied" which are two things that will stay with me for a long time to come, for a professional to say this is absolutely mind boggling but that is what she said, when that particular principle was in charge there was a lot of bullying going on and many kids were pulled out of the school because many parents did not like the methods of the principle. One of the worst ever things that has ever happened to me is when the bullying was at its worst in the last year of primary school, after our meeting with the principle when she told me that "bullying happens", bully B was not very happy with me, probably because I dared to challenge him by getting my mother down to the school to try and stop his bullying. During lunch hour that day, bully B got in my face once again and he said "you and me are going to have a talk after school", and because I drove myself home in my wheelchair I could only assume that he was going to come after me. He knew the route that I took on the way home as well because his house was on one of the streets just outside the school gate. During lunch hour and afterwards I did not think to much of it because to be quite honest I was used to all the threats, when the school bell rang I noticed bully B running home and getting his bike, he then rode off into the distance and I began to get very anxious and was almost crying, I knew I would have no defence if he decided to come after me. I was very scared, mum was always waiting for me and I knew if I did not get home on time she would be very worried and I didn't want her to feel like that, your probably all wondering why I didn't just take another route home? Well because the route I took was the safest and most accessible one and I did not want to differ from that mainly because I did not want to run the risk of getting stuck on a kerb or crossing that I was not used to. Driving a wheelchair can at times be very difficult and believe it or not, the wheelchairs get used to the paths they take and the suspension actually adjusts its self to the path it takes most often. So I saw bully B taking off on his bike and I began to get very worried and I knew if he came after me I would have next to no defence if he decided to do anything, it is a really horrible feeling and I would not wish it on anyone. Bully B is such a man, not. I was very scared and then I made a decision, on the street outside of school one of my best friends sister's lived and I called in there and my mates mum just happened to be there, she could see that I had been crying and that I was clearly agitated. I asked her to walk me home because I was scared that bully B, the mother of my friend already new what was going on after having several discussions with my mum about the problems I was having at school. She decided to walk with me for the rest of my journey home, and as I expected bully B and the rest of his pit bulls came to confront me within minutes of us setting off again, but I think it was a mistake because my friends mother gave bully B one hell of a talking to and she even reported him to the police, where of course nothing was done about the problem but it was good to see bully B on the receiving end of some harsh words for once. Like the coward he is he did not have much to say, but the next day at school I was once again in the principles office and in trouble for involving members of the public in this issue, which makes me laugh because the school was not attempting to fix the problem. There were times when I just felt like I was the reason that all this was happening, I felt like it was never going to stop and in some ways I did not see a way out. Sadly this is the reality for some children around the world, they are easy targets for people like bully B and the educational system seems to want to ignore the issue rather than put an end to it. I wonder what it is going to take until the system takes this issue seriously, is a kid going to have to murder someone before people wake up? I really don't know and I am very concerned about the future in regards to the way bullying is dealt with. Nothing stopped bully B however and he continued to bully me on a regular basis, we would be around 13 now and all us boys were beginning to take a slight interest in girls for the first time, during our first sexual health class in the first year of high school bully B threw a bit of paper at me and told me in front of the entire class that I would never be able to get with a girl because I would "never be able to get it up" or be able to make love to a woman. The fact that he said this in front of a lot of girls really messed with my head. Moving from primary school to secondary school marked another big step in my life as it does for everyone, high school or college can be very intimidating when you first go there and you never know quite what to expect. High school is a completely different ball game than primary school is, the senior students are very judgemental and you feel like you have to fit in because the last thing you want to do in high school is become a loner. I managed to have a lot of friends early on because most of them were from my old school so we all made the transition together which helps make things easier. The high school I went to was in Te Kuiti as well, it was the easiest and most obvious option, I spent my college years at TKHS which is short for Te Kuiti High School, the school was pretty well set up for a student in a wheelchair so the decision to go here was an easy one. One of the most memorable moments of my schooling life happened on the very first day of high school and when I think about now, looking back it sends me into fits of laughter because I actually believed what was said. Before going to the school we met the principle during the orientation day, and he made it clear how excited he was to have me at the school and that I need not worry about the prospect of being bullied. A few days later when we all had our first day at high school, we were all up in the big assembly and one of the first things that came out of the principle's mouth was "Simply, bullying will not be tolerated in this school" he went on to say to all the parents present at the assembly that they can rest assured that their kids will go through Te Kuiti High School plain sailing and bullying will not be tolerated under any circumstances. I was not the only disabled person in the school, there was another young man in a wheelchair which became a friend almost immediately, I think the principle of TKHS was doing the right thing by tackling the issue of bullying right from the get go and when I was sitting in that assembly listening to what he had to say I believed him and was happy with his comments because he made the message very clear to everyone, however there is a big difference saying things and actually making sure that they do not happen, that's the reason it makes me laugh when I think back to that assembly because within a matter of weeks bully B was once again on my case, yes the boy just had to go to the same secondary school as I did, it is not that much of a big deal but he just seemed to follow me everywhere I went, we both had very hard feelings towards one another at this point. When I began high school I made a promise to myself that I would not put up with bullying any more and I did have a lot of anger towards bully B because his bullying had not been resolved back in primary school and as a result he thought he could bully me without any fear of being pulled up by a teacher. My first wee while at high school was an interesting one, I was very excitable and took to the extra work load like a duck on waters back, my favourite classes were English and Maths early on, and my least favourite class was Art class because I cannot draw for the life of me! It is something that I have never been very good at, I am more a writer and enjoy expressing myself through writing stories or articles, it is a great way to get your thoughts and opinions out there. Early on at high school, my English teacher noticed my talent for writing and I remember her telling me that it is a gift that I should take advantage of in the future, something that I would later go on to do. The first year at high school rolled past relatively well and I got some good marks in most of my classes, bully B was always in the picture trying to have a go but overall I had a very good year. It was around this time that I began taking an interest in girls and well, I have never been very good at getting girlfriends but at the same time none of us guys really were. That is a part of high school without a doubt the whole boyfriend and girlfriend stage and it can be a very good or very bad time of a teenager's life, it was a mixture of good and bad for me personally. I never really had a proper girlfriend so it is one of the things on the old checklist, yes I would love to settle down and get married some day and maybe have some children of my own, I think we all want that at some stage of our life. There was one girl in school that I was really interested in, I loved everything about her and she was just a girl that I was very much attracted to, I tried asking her out quite a few times but I never got the "yes" from here. It is worth a try in any case and even if girls turn you down don't let it upset you because you can take comfort in the knowledge that you at least gave it a go. My second year at high school came around in no time at all and things were a lot easier in the classroom I found, year 10 was one of the most easy and plain sailing educational years I have been through, I passed all classes with top marks. During this second year at college things were going well in the classroom but outside in the playground things were very tough, bully B was constantly in my face and his bullying was getting worse and worse. One thing that was very disturbing with bully B was the nature in which he bullied, his bullying would often be of a sexual nature, for example he would call me things like "ass bandit" and a whole lot more, bully B had a very good knowledge of all things sexual and at such a young age I cannot help but think he may have been exposed to pornography or been sexually abused as a child, I was not the only person that had the same thoughts about this kids upbringing. People say how bullies bully other people for a reason, I do not believe this for a second, but a child's upbringing can play a major role in how they act in the teenage years. I was sitting in English class one day, it was a test day so we were all concentrating and there was not much noise in the classroom, suddenly something sharp and hard whacked me in the back of the head, and it hit very hard, I turned around to see bully B laughing and another mate of his attempting to chuck something else at me, when I began to ask them to stop I got yelled at by the teacher for disrupting the classroom while bully B sat there with a smirk on his stupid little face. This was the last straw for me, I knew that I needed to take action and at the end of the class went to see the principle of Te Kuiti High School, his response was less than what I was hoping for and he said that he "would deal with it, don't worry" so naturally I had to take his word for it and continued on doing school work. The very next day we were in English once again and I was walking around the room, when the bell went to end the class as I was on my way out of the class bully B grabbed the controller of my wheelchair and sent me into the wall, the chair smacked into the classroom wall and jammed my foot between the chair and the wall, as he walked past he said "out of the way handicap" while the teacher was too busy marking the work to even notice what had just happened. So I got my chair off the wall and made sure my foot was ok, as I left the class I could see him waiting for me around the corner so I decided to walk around the other side of the school so he would not do anything else to me, there were steps everywhere and I was petrified that he would send me down the steps or something. Most of my mates had sports practice during lunchtimes so I did spend a lot of time on my own, so back to the story. I decided to walk around the other side of the school and I was driving my chair very fast, but the problem was bully B had mates doing his dirty work as well so everywhere I went I was scared of something happening, and I did not want to go and watch the rugby practice because the grass was all wet and muddy as it was the middle of winter. I was getting increasingly erratic at this point and decided not to go and see the principle again because all it did was make things worse, so I drove myself into the assembly hall and sat their crying all alone. Eventually I decided to go back outside and I bumped into a friend of mine who had just got out of detention of all places, he could see in my face that I was scared and he knew why, I didn't have to say a word. He said "right your coming with me" and I did not have much say in the matter because he wanted me to finally confront bully B, so we walked around to the area where he was waiting for me and I was almost shaking with fear. A bully is a bully, but the really good bullies manage to get inside the head of their pray and cause fear, that is exactly what bully B did to me anyhow. So my friend took me to confront bully B, like me he knew that going to the principle was useless because nothing was ever done about the issue. So we get there and bully B is there with all his mates ready and waiting to have another go, my friend wanted me to tell him how his bullying is making me feel. So I began to try and talk with bully B in a calm and reasonable matter, all it did was make him throw more hurtful remarks at me, during this whole thing my mate was getting increasingly agitated and called me away from bully B so we could have a word. I began to cry and my mate said to me "run him down", I was not wanting to resort to violence if I could avoid it, and I was scared that if I got into it with bully B he would tip me out of my wheelchair or something. It was clear at this point that bully B wanted a fight but I refused and he began to crowd me, I felt very scared at this point and my friend was getting very close to cracking. Then as I kept refusing to fight with bully B he walked away calling me "A gutless retard" and "Its time you did something hard because you handicaps live a easy life" which pushed my mate over the edge and a massive fight broke out within seconds. My friend was out of control and it took many people to get him off bully B, all I could do was sit and watch at this point because I was so upset. As soon as the fight was over all three of us were sent to the principles office like naughty little boys, everyone who was present had the same opinion about the fight and that was that it was instigated by me which is a load of baloney. So we were called into the office and the first words out of the principles mouth were "I am not putting up with this shit in my school" and he was clearly very angry, we all were. Like the little coward bully B was he immediately went on a tangent about how my friend attacked him for no reason, claiming he "just jumped me" which is very untrue, we all began to get into a big argument right there in the principles office. To make a long story short we were forced to shake hands, the principle was very unhappy that this incident occurred at the front of the school and he raved on and on about how bad it looked for people visiting the school if there was a fight going on in the school yard, I knew right then and there that bullying was never going to be pulled up and dealt with, the attitude of the principle was shocking to say the least. My friend was not happy with the outcome but we both had no choice but to let this one go, once again I was forced to knuckle under all the while knowing that bully B would be having another go at me within days, he never had any intention to stop. We will get back to the subject of bullying a little later on in this chapter, I want to talk about the system for a little bit if I may. The school system has its good and bad points, on the one hand the educational side of things it top notch and the lessons you learn during school are very important, you parents teach you all through your life and the teachers at school help as well. I learnt a lot about hard work during school, I remember in my final year I had a history assessment and it involved watching a video on the second world war and having to write the entire worded script of the hour long video, that tested my writing endurance and it would become a tool that would prove well even during the writing of this book. This particular assessment taught me a lot about having a good work ethic, without a shadow of a doubt my favourite class during high school was history, and that was because my history teacher was just the greatest, I respected and liked him so much and was very grateful for his help over the years. Apart from history he also taught social studies and photography class so I saw him around quite a lot. The great thing about history class is that you have a lot of time to talk and discuss your thoughts, because history a lot of the time has been all about opinion, I enjoyed history more than any other class because of the big long discussions we would have about wars, and other historical things. Everyone had a different opinion in history which lead to some awesome friendly debates, during my last year of school I was more successful in the classroom than I had ever been, don't get me wrong I always got good marks but in 2008 I stepped up a gear academically. One thing about Te Kuiti High School was that it was very hard to get rewarded for your hard work, I was awarded prizes at prize giving in the junior years but during the senior years I received no reward for my hard work. In my final year I achieved NCEA before most of my friends, got merit and excellence on numerous assessments throughout the year and when it came time for prize giving my name was not read out in the list of winners, in 2008 when this happened I was very angry because I had exceeded all expectations and people who were under my level of achievement were getting prizes left right and centre while I was being overlooked. You were never rewarded for your hard work. I cannot say enough for the educational side of Te Kuiti High School because it was top notch, but as I got older and more senior in the school I was getting increasingly frustrated with this system, and when I say that I mean the disability service that the school offered. Let me try and break this down for you all, when you are a disabled student you have what is called a disability teacher who basically deals with all the paperwork and arranges any special classroom help that a student may need, for example organising a teacher aid to be a writer for the students during long assessments or exams. That side of everything is good but I am not happy overall with how the "professional" people at Te Kuiti High School treated me. My special needs teacher was very good but she just did not give me room to breathe at school, everything I did I was questioned about which lead to many arguments between me and the special needs teacher. All I wanted to be was a normal student day in day out but she made sure that did not happen. One of the most major problems I had at Te Kuiti High School was understanding, every time I wanted to see the principle I could not do so without the special needs teacher having to be present, to be honest I don't think that the principle had much confidence and needed her present to back him up all the time. I have to confess when I first met the principle of Te Kuiti High School I thought he was a genies, he seemed to be right on top of bullying and he was very assuring in the early days and I felt confident that he would make sure that people would not bully me in my time at Te Kuiti High School. As the years went on I noticed that the principles methods of dealing with bullying were not effective and if anything when I went to him about a issue he did not deal with it, most of the time he would say "ok I will deal with that" which means nothing. The next day the bullying would get worse so clearly he was not doing what he claimed to. As people I think we all get bullied at some point of our life, some worse than others. The final year at school, despite the fact that achieved well in the classroom everything else was pretty crap for the entire of the year, I learnt that some people were not the people they claimed to be and had no problem stabbing me in the back whenever something better came along, it was also quite a bad year for me health wise and things were getting harder and harder to manage, I was put onto a drug from a doctor and it played havoc with my forearms and it made me put on a lot of weight, which of course lead to more bullying at school. It was also a year of arguments, the stress of school and all the frustrations were creating arguments between my mother and I about me going to school in the morning, I began getting very angry and erratic in my behaviour. Mum and I would get into big arguments about wether I was going to school or not every morning and then we would not talk to each other until she dropped me off at school, I did not want to be at school anymore and mum did not want me there either but she knew how well I was doing in the classroom and she wanted me to capitalise on that and not just become a bum sitting around at home, which at the time really angered me. My mum made me think about a lot of things during this time and I thank her for being firm with me at times because like me, she did not want me to give in to all the bullying. I am not going to lie people, there were times when I just did not want to be this earth anymore and I could not see things getting any better, I cannot give the credit to anyone else but mum and dad for getting me through it. One of the worst things that ever happened surprisingly was down to the principle and management of the school, in early 2008 I was given a different wheelchair to trial and for some reason the chair kept braking down and we had no idea why, due to this happening I missed around a week of school. When I went back to school the chair was giving warning signs of playing up again and with this in mind I decided it may be a good idea to get myself home before doing so, because I wanted to save mum the stress of trying to push the wheelchair inside as it is very heavy. So I looked at my school timetable and found I had an important class next up, using my head Ii went to see the teacher of the class to explain the situation and ask if there was any work that I could take home so I did not miss anything. The teachers reaction shocked me to the core, she said "don't go home Michael there is nothing wrong with your wheelchair and stop saying its braking down as an excuse to get out of school". I could not even speak to her I was so shocked. As I predicted the wheelchair did brake down and I was very unhappy because I could have saved mum a whole lot of work. When I told mum and dad what was said they were fuming. I cannot write in here what they said they were so angry all sorts of words came out of mum's mouth when I told here. It just goes to show how stupid some people can be, especially when they should have a little understanding, all they had to do was look at the bloody wheelchair to see it was not working like it should. In my opinion that is not a professional. There were two incidents in 2008, my final year at Te Kuiti High School, that made me begin to consider that maybe it was time to move on and look for other things. The first of which was something that too this day still has a slight effect on me, when I think about it I get very angry because this was a case of someone who claimed to be my friend once upon a time. Let me try and paint the picture for you. I was friends with a younger girl who was the sister of a girl in my year whom I was also friends with. The younger girl was 13 years of age, at the time I was 16, I want to make it clear that me and this young girl were only friends and we had begun hanging out quite a lot. One day I was driving around the school and I ran into the older sister and I asked if she knew where the younger girl was because I had to show here something, the older sisters response was "leave my sister alone" and I was very shocked because me and the girl were only friends and to be honest we had been having a lot of fun together, but I did not listen to that comment and continued to hang out with the young girl. We were hanging out almost everyday at this point and one day I decided to ring her up at home and see if she wanted to hang out that night, the young girl said she could not because she had swimming and everything was good. Within minutes I got a very aggressive text message from the older sister, saying "stop stalking my sister". When I saw this text I flipped out and got back on the phone, I asked the older sister what she was on about and she said "If you don't leave her alone I will go to the principle" and my response to her was "go ahead" because I knew I had done nothing wrong and for one of the first times I decided to stick to my guns and stand up for myself. Then the next day I at school was probably the worst day of my life, even thinking about it today gives me chills. I walk into form room, the older sister is there and clearly not happy with me judging by the look on her face, she did not say anything to me but she could have killed me with the look she was giving, I continued to ignore her not letting anything that had been said or done make me back down, I won't apologise for being friends with someone especially when that someone treated me a lot better than most at that school. Lets be honest. Then before I knew it I was being called a stalker by many girls in my year, to be labelled a stalker because of a girls stupid little comments she made to a friend really bugged me and I don't think she knew what she was doing, it would have been a spare of the moment comment which in the end went on to embarrass and humiliate me in front of all my friends. As a result my friendship with the younger girl was basically ruined and we both felt uncomfortable, all the older sister managed to do was make my bullying ten times worse than it already was, I was friends with a younger girl well god save me. One thing I learnt at Te Kuiti High School was it is perfectly alright for a younger girl to be interested in a older guy but when the tables are turned some how you are called a stalker and other horrible things, because of the sister's stupid immaturity when it was clear I was only friends with the younger girl, my school life was damaged once again and this time way beyond repair, I knew right then and there that I could never return to the school for my final year, not with the sudden reputation I had designed by a silly, immature little girl who stupidly enough I once called a friend of mine. I have NEVER in my entire life felt the urge to be violent towards a female but there were times in the last few months at Te Kuiti High School that I wanted nothing more than to strangle the life out of the older sister. The other reason why I think made people believed what she was saying, was that she was a very high achieving student and was very popular in the eyes of the principle. When I went to his office to explain what had happened and how I was feeling he just said "are you sure? I don't think she would do that Michael", so what was I meant to be making all this stuff up? I don't think so sir. The matter was never resolved. The decision of wether or not to go back to Te Kuiti High School for my final year, year 13, was one that I had a lot of trouble in deciding what to do. I had many discussions with both mum and dad about if I should go back or not. On the one hand it would be good to live out your senior year but on the other I just could not take anymore bullying and it was clear that I no longer had the confidence of the principle, plus with all the "red tape" in the school regarding my disability and all the policies I had to follow, I decided to leave Te Kuiti High School and I decided just three days before the new school year began. So I went to get my leaving form, and during the signing process me and the principle had a chat about my time at school, in a way I think maybe he was trying to apologise because you could see in his face that he did not want me to leave. I am going to share something with you that not even my parents know about, during the process of signing the leaving form the thought did run through my head of tearing it up and changing my mind, because I kind of felt like I was running away from all the bullying when maybe if I stayed and continue to fight it, maybe it would have gone away and the new school year would be different. I knew though that is was just the right time for me to move on, I decided to go and study at the local Wintec for the next two years doing computer and business studies both of which I was successful at. I learnt a lot during my school years and I am very thankful to those who helped me out both in the classroom and on the outside of it, I have no doubt that the majority of people only meant the very best for me. I learnt so many things, and I did so much growing especially during my time at Te Kuiti High School. Bully B bullied me everyday for eight years, so naturally I have some very hard feelings towards him even now, but deep down I think he was just a very mixed up young man crying out for help. School was now behind me, and I was a changed Michael Pulman. I want to thank my parents for being there every step of the way, without them I would have gone crazy. They really are great parents, the best in fact that anyone could possibly ask for because you know that they are always there, which when you are going through the worst stage of your personal life can be and was a major help. A successful yet very painful chapter of my life had now ended, and another one was right around the corner from opening. It was my time to shine.

Chapter 6: Accepting The Realities

The school years although very successful in the classroom were difficult at the best of times. Life was going good at this point however and making the move to tertiary education was a good move for me and I learnt a lot, the world outside of school is very different and much more enjoyable I found, not to say that it is easier either. In tertiary education it is very much about self drive and no one is going to be there pushing you to do the work, you have to take on a more mature way of thinking which suited me down to the ground because it was something I had wanted for a very long time, to make my own decisions and not have to go through other people like I did back at school. Your world is in a way very limited for the duration you are at school but when you get out into the big wide world you realise "hey, the world is my oyster" and often the possibilities are endless depending on how you look at things. The first year away from school was one of the best years of my life, I learnt a lot and matured big time, and for the first time I felt like society accepted me and my disability. When I say that I mean, when I was at school I was constantly judged and mocked, when you have that on almost a daily basis you feel like everywhere except home is a struggle, during the school years home was my safe place and it was the only place that I felt normal. However tertiary education opened up a whole new world for me and before I knew it I was making friends left, right, and centre which boosted my confidence no end. Tertiary education is a lot more relaxed than high school for so many reasons, you are not constantly being nagged by teachers or worrying about the time you get to class, there is no such thing as detention which I am sure is a plus for a lot of people. My time at Wintec was self driven and I knew that I would have to put in the work 100% of the time because unlike high school, there would not be someone behind me all the time pushing me, not that I needed that mind you. I flew through my first year at Wintec and by mid October I was on holiday and having a nice, relaxing and most importantly stress free time. I remember sitting at the computer thinking one night, quite often I will sit and reflect on things and it suddenly dawned on me, on how happy I was. For the last well, five years I had been happy but always getting stomped on and mocked by stupid people, and for the first time I felt like I was normal in all parts of life. One of the biggest, no wait, yes the biggest challenges second to none that I had in my life was amazingly enough not the bullying. You would think that getting bullied and mocked almost every day because your "handicapped" or "retarded" would be a massive challenge to deal with, it was a challenge but the biggest challenge I have ever had to try and topple is the acceptance, accepting the way I am. For my entire life mum and dad have never made a single reference towards my disability in bad way, the extended family have never had a problem either which is awesome, they are truly a great family and I have been lucky in that respect. However I have discovered in the last nineteen years that some people do indeed feel uncomfortable with disability, which is totally fine with me because at the end of the day people are entitled to their own opinions. Thankfully not many people feel that way these days but during my journey I have come across a fair number of people that simply don't understand disability or they feel some way uncomfortable around it. Simply put that is their problem not mine and I am totally happy with the way I am and if someone has a problem with that well that's ok, just don't tell me about it, but like I say these days people are pretty good. I think the biggest thing with people who are not disabled is understanding, and rightly so because it is hard to understand something that you don't have any affiliation or connection too. If I am down town and a little kid starts staring at me I really don't mind, mum always says to me "why don't you ask that person to stop looking at you" but in a way I actually enjoy it because you can see their little minds working whilst they try and figure it out. Some little kids even come up to me and start asking why I cannot walk like everyone else, its so cute and I enjoy telling them why, sometimes they don't understand and others they do but it is just a good feeling when a young person does that, sometimes it actually makes me feel better about the disability. All us guys in wheelchairs have been through those moments, some guys hate it but I see it as an opportunity to educate people and sometimes they are just curious, not everyone is mocking us. It all depends on how you feel about yourself. I am hopeful that in the future there will be a lot more disability awareness classes particularly in high schools where bullying is most prominent. Accepting the fact that you are disabled is like I said a very difficult thing and no none can help you with that, because at the end of the day you are the one with this condition and it can be a very long and at times painful period of ones life. Without a doubt the biggest hurdle that I have had to jump over came over the course of a few years, and of course it was the accepting of myself and the way I am. I am not going to lie it was a very long and difficult process, and this time mum and dad could not really help me. I was at a stage of my life where I was accepted in my home and in the family, but I was noticing that a lot of people were mocking me at school and it was confusing because in my eyes I was just a normal everyday person. At around age 12 I was noticing that things were beginning to change for me physically, I was losing the ability to hold my hand up in class. Don't get me wrong I knew I was disabled and how that worked but nothing had really happened to me to spark the idea that "this is the reality" in my head. The next few years my physical ability continued to go downhill. After my spinal surgery I managed to get back a lot of the strength that I lost which was very positive. Shortly after surgery I met a doctor who was foreign and he seemed to be very on to it. He was a good man but at the same time he was very pushy when it came to drugs, in the very first meeting I had with him he wanted me to get on a drug called Epilim. Usually this drug is used for people who suffer from epilepsy which for one I don't have which confused me and my family as to why the doctor wanted me too take the drug. Now when I say the man was pushy, I mean it because he just kept saying "it would be a idea to take this drug" but he did leave it up to me. I was very unsure because I did not know a thing about the drug Epilim so he left it up to us to decide. Back in those days there was not too much information around about the drug and I just had an off feeling about going onto the drug. So a year later we had another appointment with the doctor and we wanted to know all he could tell us about the drug, his answers where short including "it could potentially help strengthen the muscles" and in past try outs with the drug it had proved to be a success with people living life with physical disabilities. Having absorbed all this information, mum and dad left the final decision up to me and I made the decision to try out the drug for a one year period to see the results and I had the choice to go off the drug after that if I was not happy with the results. I got sucked in to the doctor's claims and it had a very bad effect on me to say the least. What the drug did initially to me was make me very tired and sleepy, within a week of starting on the drug I was falling asleep in class and not being able to focus on anything which made me very angry because I am usually a very active and on to it type of person. Over the next drug made me put on weight and I began losing the ability to even feed myself, it hit me the hardest in winter, when I would be wearing tops or long sleeve jersey's I would not be able to move my arms, something that had never happened before now. In the summer I developed a urine infection, which basically made me want to pee all the bloody time which when your in a wheelchair can prove to be a major problem, and I mean major. It got to the point where I was peeing every half hour which made a whole lot more work for mum and dad. It only lasted around a week but it was the single longest week of my life. The biggest thing the drug did however was alter my mood and it made me a very angry young man on occasion, mum and dad could not say anything to me without being snapped at which im sure was very annoying as this was on top of the ordinary teenage mood swings. Mum and dad noticed this because normally I was a happy and very polite so they were slightly concerned over how angry and moody I was becoming. The massive loss of physical ability over such a short period of time made us begin to think that maybe it was time for me to consider going off Epilim, in no way did it improve my physical ability and in fact it came damn close to forcing me to lose all the physical ability that I had worked hard to achieve for my entire life. I was very angry about this because I was already aware of how much help I needed with everything and to be getting worse without being able to do anything about it really got under my skin. So I made the decision to go off the drug and when the doctor found out he was less than pleased, but it was ok for him, he was not the one suffering from lack of ability. When he asked why I went off it I told him and he was not happy with me at all. When I went off the drug I felt my strength starting to come back almost immediately and before I knew it I was feeding myself again and I was back to good old happy self. As far as I am concerned I will never take the drug again and if the doctor does not like that well to bad, this man is a real drug pusher and since then he has tried to get all my friends onto it, they all refused after seeing what it did no me. I no longer see him anymore, most probably because I will not try the drugs he keep tying to put me on, which include steroids. Let it be known now readers, steroids is a big bad drug and all us people with disabilities should steer clear of them, I have a friend who is on them of which I don't agree but it is his life. The side affects can often be severe. This phase of my life made me realise the magnitude of the disability, and that my strength can be taken away very quickly. It is a very difficult thing to try and deal with being disabled, and I believe it affects everyone in a slightly different way. I remember sitting at home one day just thinking about things, like we all do, and I began crying out of no where because I was scared about the future. It is well documented that us guys with motor muscle diseases have short life expectancies; personally I have lost two friends who have the same disability as myself. Questions like "am I going to die" and "will I get very sick" run through your head. Personally I always try and keep myself busy because when I sit and think about my disability and where I am at health wise, I just cannot deal with it and it makes me very upset. All of us try and keep busy in life though. However sometimes it can be very difficult to just shut everything out, at some point in our lives you have to confront your feelings in some kind of way. The moment of a major realisation came for me when a dear and close friend of mine passed away in 2010. Matthew Hinde was a young man that I met at the first ever muscular dystrophy camp and the first thing I noticed about him was his humour, Matthew was always a very funny and smart guy who was always down to play a prank on someone. Matthew could be a cheeky young man and he played so many practical jokes on me over the years. He used to go to the same respite care house as me and Brooke so we saw a lot of each other over the years. Matthew Hinde taught me a lot in the years that I don't think anyone could have, he was so positive and happy despite being in the worst of health at the best of times. I remember back in the day, Matthew, Brooke and myself would be playing videogames and yelling at each other, doing everything that boys do. We were free best friends and there are just too many memories for me to write about here, one of the all time memories I have was when I was about to get with a girl in Hamilton and Matthew came along and ended up ruining the chances I had because in the girls eyes "Matthew is so cute". Matthew taught me that with a positive attitude you can still enjoy life even if you have a life threatening illness, even today it still amazes me how happy he always seemed. Quite often when all us guys with disabilities get together we may have a little moan or whine about our lives, especially if we are being bullied. Matthew never moaned to me once about his situation which amazed me at the time, his health was very bad for a long time and for him to be so happy gave me a lot of inspiration. Matthew was a very gentle but ruthless sole, he had no issue telling you that you're a dick or a homo, like I say he was always down for a joke. When I tuned 17 I moved to another respite house and Matthew was to young to go with me and therefore we lost a lot of our contact which was hard but we always tried to keep in touch through text or on the social network websites. Matthew would not go away to the respite house unless Brooke and I were going to be there at the same time. One day he rang me up just to double check if I was going to the house, he was a very cute and funny young man. I began to hear talk that Matthew was not feeling very well and was in hospital, this news saddened me a lot and I was texting him as often as I could. During the V8 Supercars event in Hamilton in 2010 I was delighted to see him there and he was clearly not in the best of health but like Matthew always was, nothing would stop him and he was a massive V8 Supercars fan. A lot of our friendship was based on a mutual love for motorsport, Matthew was a massive Holden fan whilst I am a true blooded Ford fan so we got into many debates over what car was the better and more powerful one. I remember talking to him a few months before he died and he was telling me that he had been in hospital and was finding it difficult to breathe at times, I think in a way he was telling me that maybe his time had come, I didn't really register what he was saying because I did not want to start crying right there and then. You could see in his face that he had been through a very difficult time, this disability can be a shocking thing at times and things can change very quickly. One day you can be in the best of health and then you can find yourself in hospital the next week, the disability is brutal and it affects everyone slightly differently but we all try and cope with it the best we can. I will never forget the day Matthew passed away, it is one of those things that will stay with me forever. Whenever someone close to you dies you can never really describe how you feel but I will try and do so. It was an historic day already because it was NRL Grand Final day which is one of the holiest days of the year for me, and I was doing my usual game day ritual, eating in front of the television when I heard the phone ring. Almost immediately after picking up the phone I heard mum start crying so I went out to see what the hell was going on, mum was so upset she handed the phone over to dad, then my carer turned up because it was shower time. Usually I have a shower at 3.30pm everyday. So I decided to check on mum afterwards, then dad walked into the room and when I saw tears in his eyes I knew something majorly bad had just happened. Mum came in and what came out of her mouth would change my life forever quite literally, she said "I don't know how to tell you this but im sorry Mike, Matthew died this morning". I cannot describe how it felt, almost like my heart had been ripped out of my chest. It did not register at first and because the carer was there I just decided to get on with the shower. Whilst sitting under the water in the shower all I could think about was Brooke and how pissed off I was at the whole situation, then the phone rang and it was Brooke. We both had a cry on the phone and I think he needed to talk to me just as I needed to talk to him, it was a major wake up call for the both of us without a doubt. That night I was trying to watch the footy and I just felt numb and sad, you sort off feel like nothing could ever be good again. The fact that Matthew was in a wheelchair just like me made things even worse, he was only 18 years old when he passed. The following week was just as tough, I basically just listened to music for the whole week trying to go over things in my head and figure out why this had to happen especially to Matthew who was a person that did not deserve this, he must have been so scared and worried before he died. It may sound a little selfish of me but I would be a liar if I said I was not thinking "what if this happens to me", all these emotions are flying around in your head on top of the normal grieving process made for a very heart wrenching time for me and I am sure Brooke was going through the exact same thing that week. So we came to the funeral and I had already decided that I wanted to speak at the service, I was feeling good about it and had good confidence that I could get up there and speak well. However as soon as we drove into the car park at the church I began feeling very sad. They had Matthew's casket on the back of a Holden V8 Ute, and we went to have a look before going into the church. As soon as I saw Matthew's casket it dawned on me and all I wanted to do is cry my eyes out, I had not really had a cry until then and to know that my mate was inside that box was very hard to deal with. The funeral was so awesome and a great tribute to Matthew, I managed to say my speech but could not help myself and started crying. I remember looking at Brooke and I was thinking "don't you ever do this to me" because if I lost him it would be over for me. Brooke is like a brother to me and we have so much in common, to be honest id rather die before him because if he passed I would not be able to ever deal with it. Accepting the realities can be a very difficult thing, I know it was for me but somehow you just have to find a way to do it, and it may sound a little bit harsh but you either make it through or you don't. I know some guys in wheelchairs that don't want to accept it and as a result they struggle to find their way in life, also the support of the family is very crucial and I have very lucky in that respect. Am I scared to die? Yes I am. Death is something I am very scared of and I never want to die because I love my life and I love my family more than anything. One of the big things I had to accept was carers, I require 100% assistance with showering and dressing, all that personal care kind of stuff. People often ask me if it is embarrassing having someone shower you, the short answer is no because it is just something that needs to be done so you might as well deal with it. Currently I have a carer called Lisa and she is very good, me and here have some very funny arguments at times but she is a very important person in my life and I thank her for all the help. One of the biggest factors of my life is of course my wheelchair, I rely totally on my wheelchair for everything. The wheelchair has given me independence and it has changed my life in a way that nothing else does, how wheelchairs are made is most interesting. My wheelchair is driven by battery power and its top speed is around 10kph which is not very fast but I don't mind that, speed is not everything. Like any form of technology wheelchairs are prone to breaking down, when this happens it is a very stressful time whilst you wait for the people to fix the chair, often it can take a fare while and usually they give you a replacement chair in the meantime. I have had five different wheelchairs throughout my life and each has been a lot better than the previous in almost everyway, usually ever three to five years you get a new wheelchair and this can vary depending on your physical needs and circumstances. The future is the hardest thing to accept I found, and the future is unknown at this point. Will I be able to have sex? Will a cure ever be found? All sorts of questions that are yet to be answered and maybe will never be answered I don't know what is around the corner. Everyday I wake up and I am ok is a blessing for me, I am not in hospital and we manage nicely at the moment and my parents think a lot the same as I do, and that is head down, bum up and deal with whatever life throws at us. I try to not think about the disability to much and I am just lucky that I have had a pretty decent run for the past few years which sadly a lot of my friends with this disability have not had, some have been in and out of hospital and others have died so I count myself very lucky. In terms of religiousness I am not really that way inclined, I do believe in god and the after life but I am not one to go to church or harp on about it like some people do, we all have choices but I prefer to keep my feelings on that too myself. Accepting that your "different" can be a challenge but it shows your character if you can accept it and move on with your life. There is one thing that really bugs me and I find it interesting, plus I cannot understand when I hear stories about people in wheelchairs that don't like to mix with other people who are in the same situation. Let me give you an example. Shortly before Matthew passed away another friend of mine, who was also disabled passed away and whilst I was very sad, I was kind off angry at the same time. I met him at a muscular dystrophy camp in 2001 and basically since I had never seen him again, he cut all contact with us kids and none of us knew why, when he died I later found out that he did not want any contact with people in wheelchairs which baffles me even today. I was told that he cut all contact because he felt uncomfortable hanging around people in wheelchairs and he "could not deal with that reminder", how do you think we all deal with it? Its not easy but there comes a point where you cannot run from the reality anymore. Personally it angers me how some people in this situation can just choose to cut contact like that, but this guy was from what I know very inspirational. If he was alive I wouldn't contact him though because it was made pretty clear how he felt about hanging around people with Muscular Dystrophy. I cannot imagine what his family must have gone through, it is horrible but something tells me he may have had an easier time if he had contact with people like myself or Brooke because it really does make things so much easier because you realise that your not the only one in this tough place, sometimes there is just nothing your parents can say and often it takes hearing someone else say "oh yeah that's happened to me to" to make you feel a lot better about things. This man loved his music and I am sure if he were around today he would be a best selling artist because he was dynamite and he could play, better than I could ever hope to. The next big thing is what is referred to as "the elephant in the room" and it is a very controversial issue, sexual intercourse is something that can destroy even the best of lives and almost everyone has a different opinion on the rights and wrongs of the act. Sex is controversial on a lot of fronts, religious groups all have their own viewpoint on it and these days teenagers are doing it left, right, and centre even at an illegal age. Early on in the teenage years I did not know a thing about sex but as I grew I was finding that I liked girls but could never get a proper girlfriend, all my guy mates would brag about this issue and naturally I was feeling a little left out. The perception of a lot of people is that because I am in a wheelchair naturally I cannot have sex, this is NOT the case at all, potentially it could be but from what I know there should not be an issue with it. I am going to be honest, I have never had sex and it is one of the "to do" things if you like. It is a hard issue for even able bodied people to deal with at times, what I am really angry about is that people at times just assume that I cannot have sex and therefore the topic is ignored in a way, which I can partly understand because once again we all have a different viewpoint on sex. The biggest question that us guys ask ourselves is "can I perform" and sadly some of us never find out, I am not trying to make a "feel sorry for me" act here it is just the reality for some of us. I cannot talk for other people here but personally if I cannot have sex it will hurt me deeply because, well I don't know really it will just crush me.

On the other side of the coin here though is relationships, relationships take time and I am very confident that I will have a girlfriend one day and perhaps have a wife and a family, but I know I am going to have to do a lot of work to make that happen and as far as I am concerned the wheelchair and disability should have no effect on those goals. In terms of sex well I simply don't know, it is something I really want to do as I think everyone does at some point in there lives but also I realise the major odds that it may not happen. People talk about how great sex is and to potentially not be able to experience that is a little heart breaking for me so hopefully I can do it one day. We will see what the future holds, I know I am good enough to get a girlfriend and for what its worth I think I would make an awesome boyfriend so overall yes it is an issue for me but I am very confident that I will achieve sex one day. All of this last chapter has talked about the acceptance process I had to go through over the last few years and whilst it was not easy at all I am very proud that I have accepted most things and been able to make the best of my situation. Once again hats go off to mum and dad for supporting me especially when Matthew died. Finally I would like to close out this chapter by saying we all have our challenges in life and we at times can all feel like life is a bastard and everything is just so unfair. The way we bounce back to life when it is hard in my opinion defines your character and I admire my best friend Brooke more than anyone, I think he is just awesome and he gives me a boost every time I talk to him and not to sound gay or anything, I love him like a brother and enjoy every moment I have spent with him in the last nineteen years. It took me a while but I managed to accept myself for what I am and to be honest if I had the chance I would not change a thing because believe it or not this wheelchair and disability has given me so much strength over the years! It has also given me the chance to educate others about disability which is something I love to do, and in my opinion the best way to do so is through entertainment. Tyson new that and I am sure that's why he made music because just like me he had a story to tell, and he certainly told that through his music that he made in the weeks before he died. Bottom line is if you can accept and be happy with yourself the sky is the limit and the possibilities are limitless in life, I learn that everyday and I am proud of myself for not letting the wheelchair get to me and making life what I want it to be.

Chapter 7: I Live For These Things

Almost everyone in life has a passion for something, for me personally I have a passion for a whole lot of things. The other thing I think everyone has at some point in their life is excitement for something, it could be anything in the whole wide world that a person may get excited about and once again for me personally I get excited about a lot of things almost every day. Almost everyone who knows me would tell you that I am a very excitable person most of the time. As I mentioned a little earlier on in this book I have a major passion for sport and in particular rugby and cricket which are two of the most popular sports in this country and in both codes we have a good rate of success over the years. I will start with cricket, in New Zealand our national cricket team, the Blackcaps are one of my major teams and I never miss a game they play. It is safe to say I am their number one supporter and I am very passionate and knowledgeable when it comes to the game of cricket. Since my earliest memory I have been interested in cricket and I can remember at the age of three or four watching the 1995 world cup with dad, we used to have a little television in the kitchen and I remember sitting on the bench helping dad get dinner ready whilst watching the Blackcaps play in the semi final of that years tournament, although we lost the game that day began what would become a long standing love affair with the sport. In those early years I did not understand much of the rules other than a guy bowling the ball and the other guy hitting the thing as hard as possible however as the years went by my passion for cricket just grew and grew every summer. In 2001 my passion turned into more of a annalistic viewership and ever since I have become a critic and very highly opinionated supporter of the game. Summer is very much all about cricket for me and then in the winter it is all about rugby and the mighty All Blacks. Rugby is our national game and it is one of the great New Zealand past times and rugby is a celebration of everything this country stands for. New Zealand made history when we hosted the first ever rugby world cup back in 1987 and to this day it is the only world cup that the All Blacks have won. Rugby experts around the world believe that is it one of the great rugby challenges for a team when they go up against the All Blacks, if you look at the statistics the All Blacks are the most successful test playing nation despite only winning the one world cup. I remember having a little rugby ball and rolling around on the floor trying to copy what my hero's on the screen were doing, I was imagining that I was scoring the winning try and then racing around the room celebrating in victorious fashion. Every young boy in this country dreams of being an All Black one day and for the lucky few that get to wear the famous black jersey they truly living the kiwi dream on all fronts. Rugby is also a sport that brings our country together through the rough times, take this year for example, when the city of Christchurch was rocked by a massive earthquake and many people believe this sparked the local rugby team to perform so well this year. Overall I love most sports, I am also a big rugby league and motorsport fan and try to catch as much of that action as I can. Sport has always captured my emotions in a way that nothing else really does, it excites me and the thing I love most about sports is seeing an individuals performances under pressure and how they react to that pressure. Sport creates moments that live forever in peoples minds and because it is competition it will always draw fans along to the games. I have been blessed with a father that is a very keen rugby and cricket fan just like myself, usually Dad and I will go to a couple of international cricket matches in Hamilton and it is also a tradition I think. One of my greatest ever memories was when me and dad went to watch the Blackcaps take on Australia in 2007, the game was so exciting and it came down to the wire. I remember seeing dad go off his trolley with excitement and usually my dad is a laid back kind of guy so seeing him getting that excited will be something I will remember forever. If sport somehow ended forever I would not be a happy boy and life would not be worth living, my greatest sporting memory was back in 2007 when the Blackcaps needed 11 runs of the last over against Australia and after hitting a six we managed to get the win, it was truly one of the greatest success stories in New Zealand Cricket history as no one predicted we would win the game and the fact that we did was awesome. As a kiwi there is nothing better than when we get a win over any Australian sporting team because the Aussies are our enemy on the sporting front. I have always been a big fan of most sports but was never really into physical competition, don't get me wrong I had seen a few boxing matches in my time but was never really interested in any sport that involved violence. In late 2008 that all changed, I was sitting in front of the TV one night and nothing was on that was really doing it for me and then I turned to a different channel where I found that there was some wrestling on the tube, I almost immediately fell in love with it and wrestling would go on to become one of my major passions and ever since I have spent every Friday night watching wrestling on the television. There is a major argument amongst people when it comes to this sport and I think it will be one that lasts forever, many people around the world despise wrestling because it is fake, everyone knows it but I watch wrestling for the share emotion that it provides. As a disabled person I think that I have such a keen interest in wrestling because of the athletic ability of all the superstars that feature in the ring, I won't tell I lie, I wish it was me in that ring holding the title belt high with thousands of fans standing behind me. The truth is wrestling is fake and almost every aspect of a show is planned or staged down to the last tiny detail. If I was not disabled and was a able bodied guy I would most probably play rugby for the All Blacks, but if the opportunity came up I would enrol intro a wrestling school all in a bid to live the life of a wrestler. Many people don't realise how busy wrestlers are these days, not only do they have their wrestling commitments but they are also required to do a lot of PR things, like interviews with the media and other promotional activities. I would love to live that life because although extremely busy, the rewards are there and it would be an awesome way to travel the world. Wrestling is also a very dangerous sport to get into because the risk of injury is a lot higher than in most sports especially with the stunts that the superstars have to do in a bid to keep the audience entertained. In wrestling there is a famous old saying that goes "steal the show", that is the goal for every wrestler and when you steal the show it means that you have a match that is the best on the card and the audience responded in the best way, it is a hard thing to explain but you catch the main points of it. Without a shadow of a doubt my favourite thing in all sport is the Haka which is performed by the All Blacks before every game, the Haka is a traditional Maori challenge and it is a very important thing in my life. The Haka is to be treated with respect by every team that is forced to receive the challenge before every rugby game, if there is one thing that gets me pumped up it is watching the All Blacks perform the Haka just before a big game and seeing the passion on the faces of the players in the team. In this life we all have something that we are very passionate about but I am very passionate about so many things that it often effects my concentration on things, I am always thinking about so many things. Music is something that we can all relate to in some way, and as I said earlier in this book music has always captured my imagination and when I listen to it I go into another world. My dad has always been into his music so in a way I was brought up with music and at about the age of 14 when I got my first MP3 Player my interest in music took a more serious turn and these days I cannot go a day without listening to music. I really don't know why I am so into music, it helps me calm down when I am angry and it also makes me think about life in general in a way that nothing else does. Once I had left school and been at Wintec for a while I was sitting outside one day and I had an idea, a crazy idea. I wanted to start making videos on the computer and share them with the world, but I had no idea what sort of videos I wanted to make. I had always been pretty good at acting during my time at school and had a knack for acting well. However I did not want to go online and do acting videos, I wanted to be real and to make videos where I give my personal opinions on things. So in September 2009 when I got my new iMac computer I decided to make a random video called "The Michael Pulman Show" and put it onto youtube for the world to see, however going into this video I had no real plan and just decided to wing it and see how it went. For the next few months I did these videos around once a week and although it was not very popular at this point I still had a great time doing them. In December 2009 I lost the login details for the youtube account and it meant that I could no longer make the videos unless I created a new account, after a month or so of making up my mind on what I wanted too do I decided to make a new account and before I knew it I was able to make videos again but that in itself provided another slight issue. Seen as though I had made "The Michael Pulman Show" on the old account I knew that I would need a new name but at the same time I did not want too have a name that was too different from the original. I wanted a name that was short and sharp. So when I made my youtube return in January 2010 the new name was "The MP Show" and I had no idea how much of a success the newly named show would become. Within weeks I starting making new friends and before I knew it I had viewers all over the world and even today when I think that people around the world, including in Spain are watching me every week, it is such an amazing feeling and I had no idea that the show would become as popular as it has. The people that I have met through this whole thing have given me so much confidence and they have helped me get my name out there and I owe them a lot, The MP Show has also provided me the chance to do many other things in the world of social media and the internet to the point where it is an everyday thing that keeps me busy like a real full time job would do. Everyday now I am sitting at the computer working on various things, since starting youtube I have made and run my own website, make professional music and write sports and videogame articles for a news website. My passion for writing knows no bounds and my skill at writing is getting better and better everyday. When it comes to writing, there are countless opportunities out there and many people want to write but are to scared to give it a go out of fear that their writing may not be good or people may make fun of it, I myself had the same fear when I began writing around a year ago and in 12 months I have gained a lot of confidence and whilst I don't think my writing is amazing I am happy that people take the time to read my work. My big break in the writing scene came early in 2011 when I was trying to decide what I was going to do in terms of study, I had left Wintec at this point and was looking to do some study from home. I was originally going to do a degree in some field of physiology but when I saw the prices for the four year course I was not so keen, I could have afforded it but if I failed the course I could never forgive myself, and also I was not totally certain that this way the road I wanted to go down. I remember talking to one of my specialists and when he found out I was doing nothing with my life at the time he was less than impressed and also mum and dad were trying to quietly tell me that I needed to be doing something with my life, because they did not want me to become a bum and just sit around home all day. I remember sitting on my computer one night and I was searching online for some sort of writing gig, I came across a professional writers and news website and it said that they were hiring. I had always been a keen writer and wanted to write about sports, like a sports writing type of job, however I had a problem because they made it clear on the job application form that you had to have some sort of writing qualification. At the time I had been writing blogs on my website about sports so I took a punt and decided to send them my work that I had done instead of a qualification which I did not have, it was a last ditch attempt to get a writing job. The next morning they sent me a contract and I got the job as a sports and videogame writer, these days I usually write articles for them once or twice a week. I love writing simply because it provides an avenue for getting your thoughts and opinions out into the world and if you can start writing blogs or dairies online then you will get attention for other writers in no time that could potentially lead to a job in the field. My advice for people wanting to get into the world of writing is to be confident in yourself and know that there is no such thing as bad writing, it is only bad if you think it is and you should be proud of yourself for giving it ago, just make sure things make sense and do not rush it. Focus is also another important thing and if you feel yourself losing focus stop writing and then try again later, it can be hard to maintain your writing focus at times and the old "writers block" will happen to everyone at some stage but it soon clears. Life is all about confidence and I believe that we all are confident at something and even if we are not, we should try new things because you never know, you may just be damn good at it. My life has been a lot of trail and error. There are so many things that I have a major passion for, it is almost impossible to write about them all. What do I want from the future with all these things? Well I am not too sure yet, I would like to become a professional writer and hopefully become known the world over in some form of entertainment. Mum and dad have always said that I have a very active imagination and it plays right into my hand when it comes to writing and the various other things that I do with my life these days. For the last year or so things have been getting busier and busier and I have been finding so many avenues to promote myself and in particular my youtube videos and my writing skill, I am very grateful to everyone who has been a MP supporter throughout the last couple of years during this social media rollercoaster I have been on. I want to try and build on all the success I have made so far and even if I don't achieve all the goals I set for myself I will be happy in the knowledge that I have put the best foot forward. There are also some things that I would like to see changed, the first and most important is to see disabled people stopped being judged by people who think that they know what they are talking about, the next thing is bullying. Bullying is never going to stop until the so called professionals in the schools actually step up and really want to stop it, you could probably successfully argue that it is not their jobs to try and stop it, I don't have all the answers but if I had one wish right now it would be too see bullying stop for everyone, not just the disabled. I am pretty happy with my life at the moment and I have learnt many lessons through my experiences over the years, those lessons have served me well and along with the values taught to me by my parents have made me the person that I am today. I believe that if you have a passion for something and you want to achieve things for the right reasons you will always achieve them, you may need a little luck along the way but as human beings we continue to defy the odds and that is what I hope to do for the rest in my life is some form. I live for three things and they are family, sport and the world of social media and entertainment. Never be scared to try and achieve, dream a little and dare to achieve is the motto I live by and so far it has served me well. Simply put, have passion and dream believe achieve.

Chapter 8: Mum And Dad

Everyone had parents, almost everyone has a family, it is just a natural part of life. Throughout our lives we talk to our family members about countless things and we all rely on our family throughout life's journey. Some families are closer than others, some people cannot go a day without speaking to their mum whilst others can go for long periods of time without even saying hello to members of their family. My family has always been a very close and comforting bunch of people, I know that if ever I have a problem I can talk to each and every one of them which is such a great feeling that it is hard to describe. Getting back to some of the earlier parts of this book, I am adopted and have never met my biological parents. My birthmother's name is Linda and there is virtually no record of my birthfather which is slightly sad but I really have no feelings for them as I have had nothing to do with them, you cannot have feelings or miss something that has never been in your life. I wonder what my birthmother would think if she knew I was disabled? I imagine it would come as quite a shock. From what I have learnt my birthmother was a very successful woman and she ran her own business and made a lot of money, she lived in Hamilton and my birthfather was from Te Kuiti which to this day is still my hometown. Not many people know about the fact that I am adopted and many of them ask if it bothers me that my birthfather came from the same town, no it doesn't and once this book is out many people from Te Kuiti will be shocked but that is ok. I have no idea if any of my blood connections are still living in this town and frankly I don't want to know because as far as I am concerned mum and dad are my true parents and just because I do not share the same blood as them does not factor in the slightest. There are so many memories floating around in my head right now that I want to share with you all, here is a good one, Sunday is vacuuming day in the Pulman household and my dad has a special connection with our vacuum cleaner that I don't think any other human being on this planet has. My dad can be a very interesting fellow and he is certain that this vacuum cleaner has it in for him and every Sunday morning I can hear dad yelling and cussing at this piece of machinery, mum tells dad that she will do the job but dad is a very helpful husband and always insists on doing it even if the vacuum cleaner pissing him off to no end, you got to love that form of commitment. My dad has to be one of the most loyal and devoted family guys on this planet, he is always there for us and he has taught me so much about the core values that a man has, my dad is the true definition of a man in every possible way and I have the upmost respect for him. Dad is a committed father to his kids and is there for them all the time, he taught me at a very young age that family is everything and you go the extra mile for the ones you love even if it may not be in your best interests. Dad was brought up in a very strict household when he was a kid and back in those days men did not show emotion because it was considered weak and you had to be tough at all times, he is one of the older kids in a very large family that we all brought up by my nana and grandad. My dads mum, nana was a very special person in my life during the early years and she was such gentle and kind person who loved her family, nana and grandad never had much money or anything flash like that but nana just lit up the room with her kindness and smile whenever you went to see her. Nana Pulman passed away in 1998 after a long battle with cancer, I wish she was still around today, as a kid I would be lying on her while she would be talking with mum and dad and nana would pat my head all the time. I miss that. Grandad was a big part of my life in the early days but I was never really close to him, he was a good guy but could be very grumpy at times like the men were back in the old days. Grandad used to teach my dad how to chop wood when he was younger and he was probably the toughest teacher that a kid could have, dad had to chop the wood right or else he would get a sore butt. My mum is most probably the most important person in my life and her parents, Nana Bet and Poppa Bob were the best grandparents that any child could ask for. Nana Bet was a very gentle, quiet lady who taught me a lot in the twelve years that I knew her, me and Betty would spend a lot of time talking about the TV programmes that we both watched and would share our opinions on the shows. Betty would always slip me five dollars every time I saw her and when she gave it to me she would give me a wink. Nana Bet died of a sudden stroke in 2003 and it rocked my world, I will never forget the phone call when mum found out and it literally turned my world upside down as death does. I miss Nana Bet. Mums dad, Poppa Bob I would say is the most inspirational and amazing people that I have ever known, he is a truly interesting and incredible man who taught his entire family so many things over the years and often he managed to do that without even having to say a word. As I mentioned earlier in the book Poppa Bob has a massive model train set in his garage and as a kid I would spend days in there playing with his trains, his model railway collection sparked another passion of mine. I love everything to do with trains these days. Poppa Bob was a very knowledgeable man and I remember having some very in depth conversations about NZ Politics and the Tax System, usually a very boring subject for most people but when Poppa talked about it he made it sound so interesting and I am very fond of those conversations. Poppa Bob was the most respected man in our family second to none and he got that respect by setting such a good example to his kids and later on in life his ten grandchildren and to a lesser extend his two great grandchildren whom he both got to spend time with before he died. Poppa Bob was a lot like my father in a way because he was never one to show much emotion and he did not want people making a fuss over him, even in the weeks before he died he wanted to put on a front like everything was ok. Poppa Bob died in 2011 from cancer, it was actually the third time he had cancer throughout his lifetime so it took the horrible cancer three times to get him into the ground, typical Poppa, tough old bugger. So now days I have no grandparents and it kind of sucks, grandparents are very important people in a child's life and I have been lucky enough to have great relationships with all four of my grandparents so I feel very blessed and lucky for that. 2008 sparked another amazing moment in my life when my sister Jenna had her first baby, Hunter was born on November 2nd 2008 and I remember the first time I laid eyes on the little man, he was so cute and my heart turned to butter when I held on to him. Being an uncle is awesome in almost every way, you sort of feel a slight pull of responsibility but at the same time it is so much fun! Hunter is now almost three years old and he is growing up so fast that none of us can hardly keep up. In 2010 Jenna had another baby boy and he was named Xander, he is now around nine months old and he is the cutest little man I have ever laid my eyes on. There is something about babies that turns me into a big softie and my two nephews no damn well what a soft touch their uncle is. Spending time with my nephews has meant so much to me over the last couple of years has given me some of the best memories I will ever experience, I love those two boys with all my heart. I guess I had better talk about Jenna for a bit, just kidding guys it would be a pleasure to do so. Jenna is now 26 years old so there is quite a big age gap between the two of us and in a way we are very close but at the same time we are different people in a lot of ways, we often have our disagreements and like the typical guy I am I never really tell her how much I love her. I love my sister more than anything and she is such a great mother to my nephews Hunter and Xander, she can be proud of herself because I am. Just two look at my two nephews you know that they are happy little boys and they know that their mum loves them more than anything in the whole wide world. Jenna is a lot like me in a lot of ways because we both have a very short fuse and it does not take all that much to get our backs up if we are not in the best of moods, and we are both very outspoken people and have the same views on a lot of things where as other things we have a completely different viewpoint. I know that my two nephews will not read this book for a very long time, probably they will not have the attention span to read a book or this size until they are in their teens but I just want to tell Hunter and Xander how much their uncle loves them, those two little boys have changed my life in a way that I cannot describe, they just bring a big smile to my face. Having said all that I do wonder at times if I will be alive to see them make their mark on life, my disability can be a ruthless thing at times and if for some reason I am no longer around when they do things like, get their first girlfriends or graduate from university, I want them to know that I will always be there in some way. My health is pretty good at the moment and I don't know what the future is going to hold for me but whilst I am on this earth I am going to take it by the scruff of the neck and make life what I want it to be. The fact that I am disabled is almost a blessing because doing things like writing this book, or getting a job will be that much more of a success because I would have done it against the odds and restrictions giving to me by this disease. If I am around in 5 years I will be happy, yes I am a little scared of the prospect of early death but everyday that I wake up and things are good is a blessing and that is the way that we must all think, we are extremely lucky to be taking life's journey and should take advantage of every opportunity that it gives us. I am very proud of how I have dealt with this disability because if I am honest things have not been to bad, sure there have been really hard times when I have felt that life has no meaning or goodness left in it anymore, but all of these experiences have made me and my family stronger and it makes me what I am today. Finally I want to dedicate this book to my mum, Nannette Pulman. Mum you are my best friend and the best mother that anyone could ask for, you and dad have given me the best life that I child could ask for and without the two of you I would simply not be around today and would not have the confidence to do things like write this book. My dad is like I have said many times in this book is my hero, he is such a committed father and husband, you don't see a lot of emotion from dad but you know that he would do anything for his family and that is the quality I love most about him. Dad has taught me that life is what it is and you just have to get on with things, this advice has been crucial in the acceptance process of coming to terms with this disability I have. I don't see disability as a problem, I believe it is just a fact and its how you bounce back to life's challenges that defines your character. I love my life and I give all the credit to my successes and attitude towards life to mum and dad. They have made me the man I am today and that is a man that believes no challenge is unachievable and there is no mountain that cannot be climbed. In fact this disability has not effected our family in the slightest, it has made us all closer especially mum, dad, and myself because we have all been through such a lot. Mum and dad you have both given up a lot for me and I appreciate that. My parents, my soul, and my heart. I simply say, thanks for the life and the continued support. Life is like a mountain, we climb it everyday striving to achieve life's goal, happiness. Whatever road life will take me and my family down, we can be happy because we know that we have each other, I am ready for the next chapter, whatever that will be. Remember that you really can achieve if you believe. Life long and prosper.